Darcy Day

HELEN YEADON

WITH GILL PAUL

When Sophie Met Darcy Day

harper
true

To Michael

The stories in this book are based on real incidents,
but names and any identifying features have been changed
to protect the children concerned.

HarperTrue
HarperCollins*Publishers*
77–85 Fulham Palace Road
Hammersmith, London W6 8JB

www.harpercollins.co.uk

First published by HarperTrue in 2011

1 3 5 7 9 10 8 6 4 2

A catalogue record of this book is
available from the British Library

ISBN 978-0-00-735424-5

Printed and bound in Great Britain by
Clays Ltd, St Ives plc

Mixed Sources
Product group from well-managed
forests and other controlled sources
www.fsc.org   Cert no. SW-COC-001806
© 1996 Forest Stewardship Council
FSC

Contents

Foreword

Sophie was a puzzle. At first glance she was a slightly dumpy girl in her early teens who wore baggy, unflattering clothes and wouldn't make eye contact with anyone. Her posture was slumped, as if she were trying to make herself as small as possible to avoid being noticed. That was unremarkable in a girl of her age, but the most unusual thing about Sophie was that she hadn't spoken for over two years. Not to anyone.

And no one could work out why. Her school work was suffering, she had no social life and her parents were at a loss to know what to do.

One day they brought her to Greatwood, the Devon farm where my husband Michael and I looked after retired racehorses.

'I hear you let local children help out with the animals,' her mother said. 'I don't suppose we could leave Sophie with you for a couple of hours to see how she gets on? She's always liked horses.'

'Of course,' I said. There was so much to be done that we were always grateful for another pair of hands.

I was just on my way to change the dressings on a horse called Darcy Day, who'd arrived a few days earlier in a very poorly condition. She had painfully swollen, infected legs, diarrhoea, and she was drastically underweight, with her bones sticking out through a dull, matted coat. We spoke kindly to her, trying to get some kind of response, but her eyes were glazed, her head hanging. She was depressed and withdrawn. She'd lost interest in everything and everybody. We put her in a stable and she slunk to the back of it, not moving when I carefully arranged a rug over her, and not even attempting to sniff the fresh hay I placed nearby.

As we walked to the stable that morning, I explained to Sophie what was wrong with Darcy, and said that she needed very special care and attention while we tried to get her on the road to recovery. Her feed and medication needed constant monitoring and the bandages on her legs had to be changed regularly. Michael joined us in case I needed an extra pair of hands to hold her while I positioned the dressings. The three of us opened the stable door and walked in, and something quite remarkable happened. Darcy pricked up her ears, looked straight at Sophie, then turned and walked over towards her. As she got close, she lowered her head.

Michael and I looked at each other in astonishment. 'That's amazing,' I exclaimed. 'Look, Sophie – she's come to say hello to you. She wants you to stroke her nose.'

Sophie stretched out a tentative hand to touch her.

'It's extraordinary,' I remarked. 'I bring her feed to her but she completely ignores me. You're the first person she's shown any interest in.'

A smile was twitching at the corners of Sophie's mouth. She gently stroked Darcy's nose.

'She obviously likes you,' Michael added, and Sophie gave a proper smile, just a quick one.

It was the beginning of a relationship that would change both Sophie's and Darcy's lives, although we weren't to know it at the time.

We stood and watched for a moment, then we started laying out the bandages, soft wrap and ointments necessary to dress Darcy's legs. With twenty horses, two goats, four dogs, umpteen chickens and a few unruly geese to look after, there was never any time to spare.

Chapter 1

A New Life in Devon

Most people plan their lives. They choose the area in which they live because it's close to where they work, or to good schools for their kids, or because they'll be near family and friends. They plan their careers, buy houses they can afford based on their salaries, and even book their annual holidays in advance. My husband Michael and I have never operated that way. More or less everything that has happened to us over the last twenty years has been the result of coincidence, or a reaction to circumstances. It has often felt as if we were being propelled in a certain direction and we just went with the flow. Perhaps the most significant feature of the Greatwood story is that it simply evolved.

For instance, we moved to Devon in 1993 largely because of an idyllic fishing trip. It was a hot day in June, the lazy river glinted in the sunlight and a wildflower meadow stretched into the distance. The only sound was the buzzing of insects and my father sucking on his pipe. I don't fish myself but the beauty of the landscape was so intoxicating that I turned to Michael and said, 'We should move down here.'

At the time we lived in the Cotswolds, where we ran a small hotel. While it was rewarding at first, we'd been getting fed up with the relentless drudgery, and an inheritance from Michael's Aunt Gladys meant we could afford to change direction. Michael loved to write and had been working for a couple of years on a children's story, which I had illustrated. If we sold our hotel in the Cotswolds and bought a place in Devon, we'd have enough money in the bank to keep us going for a couple of years until we decided what we wanted to do with our lives. And if we found a big enough place, Michael's elderly and increasingly frail mother could live in an annex, where we could keep an eye on her.

My reverie was interrupted by a yell, followed by a loud braying sound. Dad had lifted his fishing line out of the water and flicked it backwards in a long, languid cast. Michael shouted too late to warn him that some heifers had sidled up behind us and a cow complained loudly as it was hooked solidly in the rump. The heifers charged off across the field, dragging Dad's reel behind them, and we all chased after them like the cast of a Laurel and Hardy movie, with Michael and me trying to grab the recalcitrant cow and hold it still long enough for Dad to extricate his hook.

It was a warning of things to come, a message about the trouble animals can bring into your life. Maybe we should have listened. But we didn't.

After much searching, we found a house we both liked, near Dartmoor. What sold it to us was a stunning five-foot-wide solid oak door with iron studding, which led into a small porch with oak seating and a tiny room above with a diamond-paned window. The door and the porch were probably worth more than the rest of the house and the garden put together. The property was surrounded by fields on all sides, and there were several outbuildings we could renovate. That was the good news. The downside was the carnage left by previous attempts at modernisation: concrete floors, orange and green painted beams, and the obligatory 1970s avocado bathroom suite. Undeterred, we moved in, along with our four Jack Russells, and began to do it up to our own taste, sourcing original Devon slate for the floors and ripping out the ancient plumbing.

The barns were over-run by cats and kittens, some of them feral, all in pretty bad shape. Michael's daughter Clare (one of his five grown-up children) had come to help, so she and I set about rounding up these cats in order to take them to the Cat Protection League, where they could be spayed, wormed and eventually re-homed.

We caught fifteen of them altogether, and ended up covered in scratches and bites, but we knew they would have a much better future with the charity than they would have had in our barns, where they were interbreeding and relying on whatever food they could catch. And we were better off without them as well, we mused, as we applied antiseptic and bandages to our wounds.

However, Michael and I are animal lovers. I grew up on a farm in Wiltshire and Michael had previously owned racehorses, so animals have always been a part of our lives. Once we found ourselves in a country setting with barns and fields, it was only a matter of time before we started filling them. Nature abhors a vacuum, so they say.

Walking down a lane near the house one day, Michael and I heard a pathetic bleating sound and peered under a hedge to see a goat tethered to a trailer. She was white, with pricked ears, and her rope had become tangled round the wheels of the trailer so she couldn't reach her water bucket. Our neighbour, George, appeared round the corner.

'Is that your goat?' I asked.

'Bloody nuisance, she is,' he exclaimed. 'My daughter brought her home, but unless we keep her tied up she runs off and eats everything she can reach in the garden, and some of the plants are poisonous. She seems to have some sort of homing device because every time my wife plants something a bit special, she immediately finds and demolishes it.'

I knew nothing at all about goats but I felt this one deserved more of a life than she had at present, grazing on a bare patch of earth and weeds attached to a rope that was just a few feet long.

'I'll probably have to send her to market,' George added.

Michael and I looked at each other. There was something about this funny little goat that captivated me. As I watched her try to unwind the tangled tether she gazed up at me with an anxious bleat, asking me to help. She seemed quite smart. 'I think she's great, but it's a shame she can't enjoy a bit of freedom.'

Michael glanced at me with a weary expression. He knew what was coming.

'She should be able to run around instead of being tied up.'

George raised an eyebrow, clearly deciding that we were 'up-country' folk with romanticised rural notions who might just be stupid enough to take on this troublesome creature. By this time I'd made my way through the hedge and was stroking the goat's head.

'I s'pose I could let you have her, if you want,' he mused. 'Course she did cost us a bit o' money. 'Spect you wouldn't mind giving us a tenner to make up for the loss.'

Michael reached into his trouser pocket and pulled out a crumpled tenner, and George untethered the goat, whose name, it transpired, was Angie, and handed me the rope.

'There you go,' he said, and I think we caught the sound of a cackle as he disappeared off down the lane.

We looked at Angie and she looked up at us expectantly, then we took her down to her new home, where she lost no time in befriending the dogs. In fact, before long she was behaving just like a dog: coming when we called her name, joining us all for walks, and wandering into the house when she felt like it. She stole bread in the kitchen if we were foolish enough to leave it lying out, and she was even found upstairs in the bedroom a few times, nosing about amongst my clothes.

Next we decided we really should have a few hens – just enough to provide us with fresh eggs. We went to a livestock auction in Hatherleigh, the nearest village, but our lack of experience at auctions such as these told against us and we kept accidentally buying the scrawny, pecked hen in the cage next to the white silky one we'd had our eye on. Just the slightest twitch of the hand and I found myself the not-so-proud owner of yet another straggly specimen. Once the hammer had gone down, it was far too late to admit that I had bid for the wrong hen. Thereafter it was a little disconcerting to realise that the auctioneer always looked across at me when a particularly bedraggled specimen was held up to auction, waiting for my bid.

Flirty Gertie was definitely an accidental purchase. She was one of the ugliest hens you've ever seen, with dull grey feathers, a damaged eye and an extremely loud voice, especially if anything didn't meet her approval. She didn't lay eggs on a regular basis but she liked human contact and would always rush up to greet us, and she was happy to be lifted and cuddled. One of her special talents was stowing away in the back of the Land Rover when we were going out. Once, when Michael was in a bakery in Jacobstowe, he looked out the window to see Flirty Gertie holding up traffic as she pecked in the road outside, having hopped out of the back of the vehicle. Another time, she appeared in the churchyard as we were emerging from a service and it took most of the congregation chasing around in their Sunday-best clothes to recapture her. She was finally trapped in the church porch by the organist's wife, who expertly hurled her best Sunday hat in such a way that it covered Gertie almost completely, and we could pick her up with relative ease.

So we had four dogs, umpteen scruffy hens, a goat and Michael's mother all living with us. Michael's children frequently came to visit, and we settled down to enjoy life in our new home. At no time had we ever discussed getting horses. We'd both grown up with horses and loved them but we knew what a huge commitment they required, in terms of both time and money. But then we met a woman called Pam in the local pub. She had bred horses all her life and had a yearling for which she was keen to find a home.

'We'll come and have a look,' I said, 'but only out of curiosity. We need a horse like we need a hole in the head.'

Poppy was a chestnut filly with huge brown eyes and a white blaze down her face. She had a wild, feisty expression and there was something about her that made me cautious. She was pretty but she was going to take some work. Was this really something I wanted to take on?

'I think we should have her. How much do you want for her?' Michael asked, and I turned to him, open-mouthed in disbelief. Whatever happened to discussion and consensus?

I realised my instincts about Poppy were correct as soon as we got her home, when she bolted out of the trailer. As I was attempting to lead her into the field we both ricocheted up the lane from one side to the other. She was clearly wilful and hadn't had a lot of handling and, as I had originally suspected, it would probably take a while to teach her some manners. We had problems every time we moved her from barn to field and back again, but I'd had a lot of experience in dealing with youngsters and because she was quick and clever she soon began to understand the ground rules. However, she had a temper if things didn't go her way, and we had many a battle of wills.

I have never liked to see animals on their own, and Poppy needed some company. On a hunch, I decided to put Angie the goat in the same field to see how they got on, and after a bit of mutual sniffing and nudging, they became instant best pals. Angie showed Poppy how to clamber up steep banks to eat blackberries from the bush.

It was fascinating watching a horse delicately pluck a ripe fruit from its bed of thorns. Their mouths aren't precise enough and she got a few scratches on her nose but that didn't seem to deter her. The two quickly became inseparable and, ironically, the goat who used to give George so much trouble that he kept her tethered to a trailer was able to help teach our wilful horse some manners.

Despite my initial reservations about keeping horses, Poppy rekindled my childhood love of them. I'd ridden from the age of four, and had my first racehorse at the age of seven on Dad's farm. We'd taken in a lot of racehorses that were retired from the racecourse and I knew how stunning these fabulous creatures were, and how exhilarating and rewarding they could be. Poppy was too young to be ridden for another couple of years, so when Michael and I were offered a retired racehorse called Jelly, we thought it might be a good idea. She'd be equine company for Poppy to help in her socialisation and, what's more, I'd be able to ride her. At least that was the idea.

When Jelly arrived, she was a reminder that things seldom go according to plan when it comes to animals. She hated being groomed, hated having her rug changed, and would shuffle and back me into a corner of the stable whenever I attempted to touch her. She was incorrigibly bloody-minded. Not only was she awkward and grumpy, but she was also a chronic crib-biter. 'Cribbing' is when a horse places its upper teeth on a post, arches its neck and swallows air. It is believed that this releases endorphins in the brain that help relieve stress, but horses that crib-bite fill their stomachs with air, are less likely to put on weight and have a tendency to colic. It's highly addictive and once a horse starts doing it, you're unlikely to be able to stop it. What's more, it wrecks your fencing.

Whenever I took Jelly out for a hack, more often than not she would catch me unawares and dump me unceremoniously in a ditch or on top of a hedge, for no other reason except wilfulness. I would then have to wander wearily after her to try to catch her. More often than not I failed, and I'd return home to find her waiting outside her field, keen to be reunited with her pals.

'It's rotten luck that we've acquired such a bad-tempered, ungrateful mare,' I commented to Michael. 'She hates me and everything I try to do for her.'

'Oh, she's all right,' he said. He seemed to have a soft spot for her and I couldn't understand why.

'Well, you muck her out and groom her every day then,' I retorted. Michael and I don't often argue but there are times when there is a palpable tension in the air and this was definitely one of them.

There wasn't a specific moment when Jelly and I turned the corner, but gradually, over the next few months, she began to make me chuckle instead of frown. Every morning when I took in her breakfast, she pulled her ears back, rolled her eyes and made a horrendous face at me, but I learned to take it in my stride. 'Same to you with knobs on,' I'd retort. If she lifted a leg to kick me, I made a loud tutting noise and she'd stop and give me a resigned look as if to say, 'Oh, all right, get on with whatever you have to do. Just do it as quickly as you can.' We weren't going to be best friends but she had decided she might as well tolerate me.

The next addition to our growing menagerie was an Angora goat called Monty, who became fast friends with Angie, and then Michael was offered a beautiful liver chestnut racehorse called Chic, who had recently been retired. She was gentle and kind – in fact, everything that Jelly was not. So there we were with four dogs, lots of scrawny chickens, two goats and three horses. It felt right to me. Despite all the work, I liked having animals around.

We were still having endless discussions about what to do with the next part of our lives. Should we convert more of the outbuildings and take in paying guests, as we had done in the Cotswolds hotel? The animals would be a unique selling point for the right kind of visitor seeking not exactly a peaceful retreat but an entertaining break amongst animals that were all strong individual characters.

The problem with this idea was that we hadn't yet finished the renovations on the house and they were swallowing money at an alarming rate. The front door was virtually the only thing that worked properly. Making the rest of the house habitable was proving to be much more expensive than we had anticipated. Even though we were doing a lot of the work ourselves, hitherto unforeseen problems kept cropping up and resolving them made a huge hole in the budget.

Besides, did I really want to be a hotelkeeper again?

'Helen, you're happier around horses than you are around people,' Michael commented, and I had to admit he was right. Maybe that was the direction to take.

Michael and I followed racing avidly, and we decided that breeding a small number of foals from selected mares, then training them before selling them to the right home, would be an interesting and rewarding project. We were off to a good start. The highest classes of racehorse are Groups 1, 2 and 3, and the ones we had already were bred from Group 2 winners.

Michael mentioned that he'd recently had a conversation with a local farmer who was trying to sell three ex-racehorses which were in foal to a stallion that was quite popular at the time. 'Why don't we just pop along for a quick look?' he suggested. 'Just for research purposes.'

Of course, any dog lover knows that you never go along to have a 'quick look' at a litter of puppies and come home empty-handed. The same goes for horse lovers and stud farms. And so it was that we came home with three in-foal mares, each with foals at foot. That made a grand total of six horses and three foals, with more on the way. We were running out of space and had to rent another field to accommodate them.

Meanwhile, our cash flow was beginning to look a bit ropey with all these mouths to feed. 'Why not take on some kayed lambs?' my father suggested. He was a down-to-earth, Yorkshire-born man who didn't suffer fools, and he knew all there was to know about farming, so we followed his advice.

Kayed lambs are orphaned ones that can be purchased relatively cheaply, which can then be reared and sold at a profit. They'd have the added benefit of keeping the pasture in good condition. So we bought twelve lambs, rigged up a bottle-feeding system in one of the barns, and once again recruited Michael's daughter Clare to help.

By now our lives were completely full with feeding and caring for the ever-expanding range of livestock, and scraping old paint from woodwork in our spare time. I scarcely ever had time to go out for a ride, or to walk along the pretty lanes and admire the wildflowers growing in the hedgerows. One sunny day I stood back and remembered why we had come to Devon in the first place: to enjoy its beauty, to relax and decide where we were going next, to take a bit of time out. Whatever had happened to that idea?

All the same, when I opened the door at five in the morning and walked across the yard to boil up a huge vat of barley for the feed, I often found myself humming under my breath. This was a whole lot more satisfying than making fried eggs and two rashers for human guests. It may have been unplanned, but I was blissfully happy with our unpredictable, unruly menagerie.

Chapter 2

Moving to Greatwood Farm

As luck would have it, we had just finished the renovations on the wing of the house that we had converted for Michael's mother to live in when, sadly, she passed away. Michael and I were left with a rambling property that was far too big for the two of us but didn't have enough land for all the animals we had acquired. The foals were growing up and needed to be weaned, and the mares would soon be due for foaling. That meant we needed more stables and it became obvious there was never going to be enough room for us all where we were. What's more, there was a lane between the house and the outbuildings, and passing cars had to screech to a halt if Angie poked her nose through the hedge, or Poppy dragged me out for a walk. And we were overlooked on all sides by neighbours, so it wasn't quite private enough for our taste.

It was a stunning house once we'd done all the renovations, and it was a shame to leave behind all the fruits of our hard labour, but it wasn't quite right for our needs any more. We took a deep breath, sold up and moved to a new home on a nearby country estate. There we had sufficient outbuildings to stable all the horses, but the hens had to share a little brick outhouse with my deep freeze. Michael's son Tod was bemused when I sent him to fetch a pack of frozen peas one day and he had to flick off hen droppings before bringing them into the kitchen.

'I come to you for my fix of antibodies before the return to London life,' he laughed, but I noticed when I served dinner later that he stared long and hard at his plate before picking up a fork.

Our breeding programme got off to a good start, and I was involved in every aspect of the foals' upbringing. Often I was the one to check their position when the mare went into labour; one foreleg should emerge first, then the other, then the muzzle. I'd have to make sure the newborn foal could stretch up and reach its mother's teats to get antibody-containing colostrum within the first few hours. And I'd be there for the first steps outdoors and all the major milestones of its first year of life. I hated letting them go when Newmarket sales came around. They were my babies. It was hard to hand over the responsibility to someone else, but that had been the plan. We hoped that out of our very small breeding operation we might achieve a winner or two. If they did well, that would be great, but if they didn't we would stop. Whatever happened, we felt we had a responsibility for any life we brought into the world.

Neither Michael nor I are the kind of people who are driven to make a fortune, and it's just as well. Belief in what we are doing has always been of primary importance, and we tend to make decisions instinctively rather than being guided by commercial logic. We both have strengths that complement the other, and together we usually seem to make the right decisions. But the day Michael went to Ascot sales on his own, with the idea of picking up another one or two well-bred mares, I should have had an inkling that the best-laid plans can go awry. He ended up coming home not with some mares but with a discarded gelding, an ex-hurdler that had never been particularly successful on the racecourse and would have been heading for the abattoir had Michael not stepped in.

'It's one thing raising your hand by mistake at a hen sale,' I said caustically, 'but to raise it deliberately at a horse sale is something else again.'

'You would have done the same,' he told me. 'Just look at him.'

He was right. I would have.

Charlie was a sad-looking horse, so thin that his backbone was sticking out and we could count all his ribs, and he had the sour smell that we were to learn is characteristic of malnourished animals. What made me angriest when I looked closely was that someone had clipped him to try to smarten him up for the sale, and it must have been horribly uncomfortable for that poor horse to feel clippers running all over his sticking-out bones. It was shameful. We put some spare duvets under his rug to keep him warm, gave him a course of wormers, had him checked out by the vet and fed him carefully. Within three months of receiving this kind of care, he was a completely different horse. He was bay with white socks, good bones and a solid, dependable character. We found he was well trained and once he was healthy enough to be taken out hacking, he turned out to be a lovely horse to ride.

The transformation from the sorry creature Michael had brought home with him to this healthy, intelligent, good-natured animal was dramatic and it made us both furious to think that this young horse – only five years old – would have had no chance of a future. The meat man had actually been bidding against Michael in the auction. Within nine months we had found Charlie a new home where he settled in happily.

The last thing you should do as a breeder is take on 'charity cases' that drain your precious resources without contributing to the balance sheet. We kept selling our yearlings, but at the same time we could never walk away from a horse in need. We just didn't have it in us.

One day we went to buy a new trailer at a farm that was miles from anywhere. In a field nearby, we could see three horses standing around looking dejected. One in particular looked up at us hopefully and within seconds Michael had leapt the fence to go and have a closer look.

'Uh-oh, this is not good,' I thought to myself. And I was right. The upshot was that the trailer wasn't empty when we drove home later that day.

Red was a five-year-old stallion from a leading blood-line and although he wasn't in terrible condition, he was unsettled because he had been put in a field with some mares and his instinct was to keep trying to mount them. This gave us a problem, of course, because where would we keep him that he wouldn't be bothered by all our mares? Fortunately I found a knowledgeable horse-woman, Sandra, who lived near us and was happy to let him stay in one of her stables. After a veterinary check-up and a few weeks of intensive care, we found he was a happy and quite beautiful horse, with a deep red sheen to his coat. He didn't like being turned out into a field for any length of time or he would panic, but he was perfect for our mares, behaved like a true gent around them, and did his job when required.

The next horse we 'rescued' was one that I found while I was out riding Chic. As we rode through a semi-deserted, dilapidated farmyard, Chic became uncharac-teristically jumpy and unsettled, as if she knew something I didn't. An instinct made me decide to have a peek inside a closed cob barn, and a dreadful sight met my eyes: a skinny chestnut mare was lying on a filthy bed, with some mouldy old hay in the corner beside a bucket of stale, greasy water. She had dark filthy patches on her sides from lying in her own droppings and she appeared listless, with her eyes closed, even when I spoke to her.

I had a lump in my throat as I stroked her and whispered words of comfort. It was hard to leave her there, but she obviously belonged to someone and I knew I couldn't just steal her. Choked with emotion, I went home and told Michael about her, and within the day we'd tracked down the owner and agreed a deal for the horse, which was named Betty. I went back to the barn, slipped a bridle over her head and led her outside into the sunshine. She blinked hard, unaccustomed to the light, but let me lead her on the four-mile walk home, stopping every now and then to munch on some grass by the roadside. We put her in a stable next to Chic with a deep straw bed, and I could tell she was content by the way she settled down and closed her eyes. She knew she was safe.

It was gratifying how quickly horses transformed when they got decent care, turning from depressed, unhealthy animals into lively, happy characters in a short space of time. The more horses we rescued, though, the greater the financial burden on Michael and me. To try to make ends meet, I took a job as a chef at a nearby college, making lunch and tea for the students, and my days became completely dominated with producing food for animals and humans. I got up at five to do the animals first, then made my way to the college by seven. I'd cook until lunchtime then slip home for a few hours to do the housework and chores on the farm. At four I'd feed the horses once more, then return to the college at five to make tea for the students. Then when I got home at seven in the evening, I would tuck up the horses for the night and fall into my own bed not long after. It wasn't ideal by any means.

Despite this extra income, we couldn't afford to heat the whole house over the winter so we started living in our bedroom, where there was a sweet little Victorian fireplace in which we could burn coal and logs. We moved the television up there and were quite comfortable, except for the huge shock to the system when we had to use the loo or go to the kitchen to make a cup of tea. As soon as I left the bedroom, the Arctic air chilled me to the bone, and it took ages to get warm again afterwards.

It wasn't long before we felt that we were perhaps outstaying our welcome on that country estate. Despite our best efforts, the horses had been nibbling at the bark of a few of the trees on the parkland, which wasn't, understandably, appreciated by the owners. We also worried about the horses being out in the fields when there was farm machinery trundling past and umpteen different people going about their business. We noticed an advertisement in the local paper for the lease of a farm near where we had rescued Betty and when we enquired we found that it was just about affordable, because of the general dilapidation of the property. In the spring of

1995, we packed up lock, stock and barrel and moved to our new home, which went by the name of Greatwood.

Greatwood Farm was set in a steep wooded valley leading down to the River Torridge, and the farmhouse was built back into the hillside. The house was damp and unloved, with peeling wallpaper and an indescribably awful bathroom, but the farmyard was stunning, with plenty of barns, outbuildings and meadows. The tall grassy banks separating the fields were covered in primroses when we arrived, and wildflowers poked out between the cobblestones in the paths. Opposite the farmhouse, a granite track led down to some watermeadows along the riverside and in summer, when the water levels were low enough, there was a ford where we could ride across to the other side. Nothing had been touched for what seemed like hundreds of years, and to us it was idyllic.

The only drawback to Greatwood was that it was on an estate where they ran a commercial pheasant shoot, but the estate owners assured us that they would always give us plenty of advance warning when a shoot was taking place so we could take the horses indoors. We didn't want to risk them panicking and injuring themselves at the sound of gunshots.

Meanwhile our collection of horses kept growing. We were joined by Fasci, a pony with a dark coat and patchy mane, who we had seen grazing on her own in a field nearby, where she was looked after by an elderly gentleman called Peter. I never like seeing horses on their own, because they are herd animals, so I got into conversation with Peter and after a while I tentatively suggested that maybe Fasci would enjoy the company of coming to board with our lot. He agreed that she could join us, and what's more, Peter came onboard as well, spending that summer helping us to convert the outbuildings into stables and feed sheds to house our growing menagerie in the coming winter.

We now had enough room for Red, the stallion, to come back and stay with us, and I became determined to find a pal for him to stable with. Horses aren't usually happy without companionship. It would have to be a small gelding, I decided, with sufficient character to withstand any amorous advances from the lively Red. As luck would have it, I heard about a miniature Shetland pony called Toffee that needed a home. Would Red let a pony share his stable? It wasn't a conventional pairing and it was with a certain amount of apprehension that we introduced them.

We were pretty confident that Red wouldn't attack Toffee outright, but nevertheless we stood nervously by with head collars, ready to jump to the rescue if needed. For ten seconds there was silence, then Red let out a roar and tried to scoop Toffee up under his front legs. We were just about to dive in and separate them when Toffee turned, kicked out at Red with both hind legs, then began to explore the surroundings. Instantly Red's body language changed, and he approached Toffee again with a little more respect and wariness. Toffee ignored his advances, and was clearly quite unfazed by the whole encounter, despite the fact that he was only 28 inches tall, while Red is a thundering Thoroughbred stallion of 16.2 hands (equivalent to 64.8 inches, so more than double Toffee's height).

We continued to watch for several hours in case the mood turned nasty. Red was fascinated by Toffee now but kept a safe distance from those flying hind feet. As night drew in we decided we should separate them so we could get some sleep without worrying. We put a head collar on Toffee and started to lead him out of the door, and suddenly all hell let loose. Red threw himself around the stable, roaring and screaming, distraught at being separated from his new companion. There was nothing for it. We had to bring Toffee back and I spent a long, uncomfortable night on top of a raised platform at one end of the barn, from where I kept watch on the two of them as they snoozed down below.

The next day, when we turned them out in the field together, Red hurtled round chasing after Toffee but he was met with the same calm indignation as before and he retired sheepishly. They were getting used to each other, though, and it wasn't long before they were firm friends. In fact, Red often started panicking if Toffee wasn't in sight for some reason. Within a week they were inseparable.

It was the first instance of my 'matchmaking' at Great-wood but by no means the last. Stabling the right horses together made our jobs so much easier that it became one of the most important, and fascinating, of the challenges we faced. Sometimes it worked, sometimes it didn't, and it wasn't always the obvious matches that worked best.

Betty initially found the move to Greatwood disturb-ing, because she obviously remembered the bad experi-ences she'd had in that part of Devon. As we unloaded her from the trailer, she became wide-eyed, started snorting and shook from head to hoof. Thankfully, she had had time to get used to the other horses, and was especially close to Chic, a particularly calm mare, so she took the lead from her.

We'd sold the lambs but we still had our hands full tending the horses, goats, chickens and dogs, so we were more than happy when the local Sunday school started sending children to help us out at weekends. I've never been a kiddie-oriented person. I expect them to behave like mini-adults and treat them that way. Despite having five of them, Michael is the same. But the children who came to help at Greatwood were a terrific bunch, who were very helpful to us in mucking out, collecting eggs, sweeping the yard, grooming horses, and all sorts of other tasks. They never misbehaved because there was a certain healthy fear of the huge racehorses clopping around. They paid attention to instructions and were very careful whenever they were in the vicinity of the animals.

I was fascinated by the way the animals responded to children. Even the stroppiest of our horses, such as Jelly and Red, would greet them by lowering their noses so that the child could reach up to give them a stroke. They were careful not to stomp around when a child was in their stable, and stood still when they were being groomed. If only they'd done the same for me, life would have been a lot easier.

Several times Michael and I stood back and marvelled about how calm and gentle they were with children around.

'Shame they're only here at the weekends,' I said, without any idea how prescient the remark would be.

Chapter 3

Flat Broke

During those first years in Greatwood we had about twenty horses to keep, along with goats, dogs and chickens, and our money was dwindling fast. I took a part-time job as a dinner lady at the local school, where I was shocked to find they never cooked any fresh produce – it was all ready-made meals straight from the freezer. Years before Jamie Oliver came on the scene, I battled the system and managed to get some local suppliers to deliver seasonal fruit and veg for the children, although it didn't do me any favours with my supervisors.

My paltry earnings weren't enough to keep us afloat, though, and gradually Michael and I began to sell off any possessions that could raise money. We got to know an antique dealer in Taunton who bought some pieces from us, including a gold bracelet my grandma had given me just before she died, and Michael's father's watch – both of which were very hard to part with. Even the dealer had tears in his eyes as we handed them over.

We had some inherited family silver and Michael decided to travel up to London in the hope of getting a better price for it there. He set off on the train, clutching a large holdall full of silver salvers, bowls and goblets, and made his way to a smart shop in Bond Street that we'd read about in the newspapers. He straightened his tie and brushed down his collar before walking in and placing the holdall on a counter.

'Are you interested in buying some silver?' he asked, unwrapping a couple of the items on top.

'Plate,' the man said, after a quick glance.

'Pardon?'

'They're silver plate. Not solid silver.' He picked them up and turned them over. 'Not inscribed either. They'd have been worth more if they were.'

He made an offer for the lot that was only a fraction of what we'd thought they were worth, but with the rent overdue, and having come all that way, Michael felt he had no choice but to accept.

We didn't tell our families about the trouble we were having but they must have realised, because every time they visited us another antique chair would be missing from the sitting room or there would be a rectangular space on the wall where a picture used to hang. My father dealt with the problem in a typical brusque farmer's style:

he gave us forty of his ewes and bought us a couple of Sussex rams to go with them.

'Thanks, Dad,' I said doubtfully.

He meant well, but it was then that our nightmare with sheep began. The soft, wet ground at Greatwood meant they kept getting sores and infections in their feet and needed to be rounded up daily for treatment. Some silly blighter would get its head stuck in a fence the minute you turned your back, while another would roll over and be unable to get up again. The rams were even worse. As soon as we set foot in their field they would charge at us full pelt and we had to hurl ourselves out of the way at the last minute to avoid being sent flying. Despite being a farmer's daughter, I'd had no idea how high-maintenance sheep were. They really did seem to have a death wish, getting themselves into life-threatening situations on a daily basis.

The next money-making scheme was suggested by a chap called Stan in the local pub, who persuaded us to buy thirty goslings from the market, raise them, and sell them just before Christmas. We put them in a field to graze, not realising that they would have to be brought indoors and fattened to get them to the size customers expect of their Christmas roast. When I eventually tried to feed them up, too late in the day, they turned up their beaks and refused to eat anything at all. I had to cancel our Christmas orders and eventually passed most of them on to the Goose Rescue Centre, apart from five that we kept.

Amongst those five was Horrible Horace, a deformed goose my brother had dumped on us. Horace may have been crooked and bent, but his disability didn't stop him flying at any children who came nearby. He thought he was a dog and would rush up to greet visitors, honk whenever the dogs barked and accompany us on walks. All our attempts to pass Horace on to other people failed, so we were stuck with yet another difficult, eccentric, bloody-minded animal to care for.

As if our financial troubles weren't enough, word began to spread that we were prepared to step in and help with sick, temperamental or abandoned ex-racehorses. It seemed there were lots of people out there desperately trying to find a home for horses that were too old, past their prime or that hadn't ever fulfilled their potential. Thoroughbreds need experienced handlers because many of them are unused to being ridden by anyone but a professional jockey and, what's more, they are expensive to keep. Many of them need to be reschooled if they are ever to have a second career, but this took time, money and expertise.

Michael and I couldn't possibly accommodate every single horse that was offered to us, but we spent hours on the telephone giving advice and trying to find potential owners for each animal, because the alternative was too awful to contemplate. For such beautiful, intelligent animals to be discarded simply because they couldn't run fast enough was not morally acceptable.

As a farmer's daughter I know there are hard realities to be faced in livestock breeding. My blunt Yorkshire father once said, 'The very word "livestock" implies "deadstock" and if you can't handle it, you'd better do something else with your life.' But my heart always melted when a seriously ill or badly treated horse was brought to us. I could never turn them away.

In the first year at Greatwood, there was a mare called Kay whose owner hadn't been able to afford proper medical care for her. Kay was in a lot of pain when she came to us and kept trying to kick up at her stomach. The owner said she'd tried to train her out of kicking herself but to no avail. But why was she doing it? What was the problem? I called the vet, who detected a sizeable growth in her stomach, and told me that sadly it was inoperable. There was nothing he could do. It was a horrible night, with rain lashing down and gale-force winds ripping around the barn. We had no alternative but to have Kay put down, with the other horses standing round watching. There was a collective whinny as she fell to the floor and a few came over to sniff her but most carried on eating their hay. They didn't know her, so weren't directly affected. As we left the barn, I felt unutterably sad for that poor horse, who'd obviously been suffering for some time. Vets' bills are expensive. That's why we had to be sure that when we rehomed horses, we only did so with people who could afford to keep them properly. We couldn't risk any horses that passed through our hands ending up like Kay, or Betty, or Charlie.

Our own financial situation went from bad to worse. Each new bill was greeted with much head-scratching and the scribbling of frantic sums on the backs of envelopes, and every month rent day loomed like a sick headache. How had we got ourselves into such a pickle? The inheritance from Michael's aunt and the money from the sale of our house had long gone, and we had very few, tiny sources of income. Then one day, I got a phone call that gave us a glimmer of hope.

'My name's Vivien McIrvine,' the voice said. 'I'm Vice President of the International League for the Protection of Horses. I've been hearing a lot about you and everything you are trying to do for racehorses and I wanted to tell you that I'm full of admiration for the work you're doing.'

'Thank you. That's good to hear. But I'm afraid it's just a drop in the ocean.'

We chatted for a while about the horses we had at that time, the ones looking for new homes and the ones we'd managed to rehome already, then she got to the purpose of her call.

'The work you are doing with racehorse welfare is invaluable and rare. You must carry on and, as I see it, the only way that you can do that is if you put it on a firm footing and become a registered charity.'

Michael and I had already been considering this option but the call from an icon of horse welfare pushed us into thinking about it more seriously. It was a great compliment to hear of her admiration for our work and for a few days afterwards we mulled it all over. We knew there was a chance our application wouldn't be successful anyway, but if it were, we'd become accountable to the charity commissioners and would have to be much more professional about the way we managed what had been, until then, an instinctive kind of operation. But we really had no choice. We had already become heavily involved in not-for-profit work on behalf of ex-racehorses by funding it all ourselves, but we couldn't go on like that because our funds were rapidly evaporating and we would have become insolvent. That would have brought an end to our work and most certainly an end to the lives of the horses in our care.

Decision made, we started the lengthy process of applying to be a charity, which initially involved filling out an extraordinary number of forms. We were warned that the granting of charitable status could take a while – always assuming our application was approved – but it felt like a step in the right direction.

We had decided some months before this to stop breeding horses. We had only bred a dozen or so before we realised there were too many being bred that didn't ever reach the race course, either because they weren't fast enough or for some other reason. There was no organisation in place to care for these unwanted horses and, at that time, no one was encouraging ordinary horse owners to take on a Thoroughbred. By breeding horses, we were contributing to the problem and as soon as we became aware of this, we stopped.

In the meantime, we had four mares that were all due to foal around the same time, and umpteen ewes that were due to lamb, which meant a couple of months at least when Michael and I would have to survive on very little sleep. Fortunately we have entirely different sleep patterns. I rise early and go to bed early, while he's the opposite, so we agreed that he would sit up with them until 2am then I'd take over from 2 until morning.

Sometimes foaling was reasonably straightforward, but when it came to Chic we were in for a marathon. She was in labour for hours, the foal wasn't in the correct position and we had to call the vet to come and turn it. Out it came, tiny and weak, but Chic was still in labour and we realised she had a twin in there, which was eventually born dead, about the size of a cat. The first foal was very weak and didn't have a sucking reflex so we had to tube-feed him. He was shivering with cold, so I got one of my jumpers and threaded his tiny front legs through the sleeves, then I wrapped tinfoil round his back legs to try to retain the heat. He was a poor little creature. Chic licked him gently, every ounce the loving mother.

For three days we nursed that foal day and night, and on the third day we were heartened when he managed to get to his feet and stagger a few steps on what were impossibly long legs for such a tiny chap. Chic stayed very close, watching what we were doing and letting us milk her, but she didn't try to intervene. She knew we were doing our best. Then on the fourth day, the foal's breathing became laboured. I sat down beside him, put his head on my lap and whispered to him gently as he passed away in my arms. There was a huge lump in my throat. He'd struggled valiantly but was just too weak to live.

I felt so sorry for Chic. She'd been good and patient, and we'd all tried our hardest, but it wasn't to be. She kept nudging the foal's body, trying to get it to move, so we left her with it for a few hours so she could understand he had gone.

It would have been a crying shame if no good had come out of the experience so we asked around and found out about a local foal that had lost its mother, and we took Chic over to see if she would adopt it. We used that classic country trick of skinning Chic's dead foal and placing the skin over the live one so that Chic would believe it was her own. Chic took to the new foal with alacrity, proving to be a most diligent mother, but Michael and I were pretty sure she wasn't fooled. She knew her foal was dead and that this was a new one, but she made the decision to adopt it anyway.

No sooner was this drama over than the sheep started lambing and we had to sit up all night long to make sure the lambs emerged safely and weren't then attacked by rats. It brought back many memories for me of watching my father presiding over lambing at the farm where I grew up. Once when I was just three years old, I watched him pulling out a lamb that wasn't moving and he smacked it hard several times until it began to bleat. It obviously made an impression on me because at dinner that night, I told my mum: 'That was a naughty lamb that crawled into its mummy's bottom and Daddy did smack it hard.'

As soon as the lambs were big enough, we sold them, along with the rest of the flock (bar two), and, unlike the horses, I was glad to see the back of them. Sheep are a law unto themselves, with very few brain cells to rub together. Give me horses every time!

All the time we were firming up and clarifying the plans for our charity. There were already organisations out there dealing with poorly treated welfare horses. We wanted to focus on horses that were retired from racing while fit in body and mind, horses that we could retrain and pass on to good homes. The charity would retain ownership of each horse so we could check up on them and bring them back if the new owners were no longer able to keep them. We chose some trustees – Father Jeremy, the vicar at St Michael's church just four miles away from Greatwood, and Alison Cocks, the woman whose orphan foal had been adopted by Chic. She had a profound knowledge of racing and horses, and we sang from the same hymn sheet when it came to horse welfare.

Next, we had a visit from two charity commissioners – men in suits who delicately picked their way over our cobblestones trying not to get anything nasty on their highly polished leather shoes. They interviewed Michael and me at length, being particularly concerned to establish that we were in it for the long haul. We knew this was serious. The charity would have to be run properly, with full annual accounts, and we would be guardians to all of the horses that passed through our care. When the commissioners finally left, they gave us no clue either way as to whether our application would be successful.

It was several months later, in August 1998, that we finally received a letter saying that we were now a registered charity, and giving us our charity number. It was just over three years since our move to Greatwood and it seemed somehow fitting that we should name the charity after this farm, where our work with ex-racehorses really started, and where we had already achieved some notable successes.

Vivien came to help us design all the forms we would need, such as the gifting forms that would have to be filled in by anyone who sent us a horse. This was designed to avoid a scam whereby someone could bring us a horse in very poor condition, let us pay all the vet's bills and nurse it back to health, then return to claim it back again. With our contracts, we took on a duty of care for life, and even after we rehomed a horse we had the right to check up on it at any time to inspect its living conditions and general health. If a home check didn't come up to scratch, we'd take the horse back again. It was our responsibility.

We wanted a Greatwood logo and were delighted when a funding trust gave us a grant that allowed us to employ a marketing company to design one for us. They came up with all sorts of ideas before a chance photograph taken by a local reporter provided the inspiration. A girl called Jodie had come to us for work experience and the photo caught her in silhouette as she looked up at a Thoroughbred. The image seemed perfect and worked well for the farm sign, letterheads and business cards. Little did we suspect at the time how relevant the juxtaposition of a horse and a young person would turn out to be.

Soon horses started arriving thick and fast. Sometimes the RSPCA or another official charity asked us to step in, but on other occasions individuals just arrived on our doorstep with a horse in their trailer. Once we were brought nine horses in one delivery, all of them collected from an owner who hadn't been taking proper care of them. We had to divide up our barns with partitions to keep the mares separate from the geldings, and our workload increased all the time.

It was a life I loved, but some family members found it difficult to comprehend. My father had only recently retired from a career as a very successful farmer and he thought we were mad. 'You'll never get rich like that,' was his attitude. 'So why give yourself all that work?'

On one visit he watched me nuzzling the horses as I walked through the stable and looked thoughtful.

'Did I ever tell you that your grandfather used to train horses for the army during the First World War?'

I vaguely remembered hearing about this, and asked for more details.

'He was awarded a medal for bravery. Once a cart carrying munitions was hit and your grandfather wriggled out to unharness the horses pulling it, despite the fact that he was under fire.' Dad nodded. 'I suppose your love of horses might have come from him. That might explain it.'

I liked that thought, but in fact I think it was all the horses I grew up around that gave me love and respect for these intelligent, sensitive creatures that all have unique personalities. I learned to ride when I was four, on a pony called Tam O'Shanter, but the horse I was most in love with as a child was called Shadow. She was an ex-racehorse, very feisty and wilful, but such a gorgeous animal that I fell madly in love with her with all the passion of youth. I poured my heart out to her on our long rides round the estate where my family lived. There was a big ornamental lake there and Shadow loved the water, so in summer I used to let her trot in and I'd slide down off her back and hold onto her tail as she pulled me along, deeper and deeper across to the other side. She was my best friend from the age of about seven to ten. I was closer to her than to anyone else, and I have wonderful memories of our adventures together.

Michael's elder daughter Kate has two boys, Will and Alex, and they used to come and stay with us during their school summer holidays. It was lovely to see them bonding with our horses and I always encouraged it because I wanted them to experience some of the magic I'd had as a child. If there were any foals, we let the boys name them, and they opted for several non-traditional horse names, such as Miriam, Marcus, Wilbur and Doris. No matter. I loved seeing them having fun and learning to love horses as I did.

The family complained about conditions in winter, though. It was a particularly wet part of Devon and it always seemed to be raining, meaning the yard became a sea of mud. Inside the house it was bitterly cold and hurricane drafts swept through the ill-fitting windows. Fireplaces smoked, the walls were damp, and the only way to survive was to wear umpteen woollen sweaters one on top of the other.

One year, the family came for Christmas with us and got a taste of our lifestyle that they didn't much appreciate after a bay mare called Nellie fell ill on Christmas Eve. I knew at a glance that it was colic so we called the vet, who came out to treat her and told us to keep an eye on her overnight. Colic is a nasty thing, sometimes caused by an impaction in the gut. It can either be cured more or less instantly, or it can develop into something much more sinister. It's important to make sure the horse doesn't roll over, resulting in the further complication of a twisted gut. All night I walked poor Nellie up and down the lane in front of the house to try to distract her from the pain and stop her rolling but her whinnying kept everyone awake. Towards dawn, her condition deteriorated and I had to call the vet out again. We rigged up a drip to treat her in one of the stables but, despite our best efforts, she became toxic and had to be put to sleep. I was completely distraught, as well as shattered from lack of sleep.

When the children woke on Christmas morning, we had to break the news to them. I went into their room and was surprised to see clingfilm all over the windows.

'What's that doing there?' I asked.

Kate explained that the bitter north-easterly wind had made temperatures drop to sub-zero and it was like trying to sleep in a draughty igloo. They didn't want to disturb us and clingfilm was the only thing they could think of to provide a modicum of insulation.

I told them about Nellie and comforted the boys as best I could, then it was time to rush outdoors again for the morning routine of feeding and mucking out. Animals don't know that it's Christmas, after all. Late morning, I was sweeping the yard, trying to keep busy to stop myself brooding about Nellie, when Kate popped her head out the door.

'Erm, Helen …?' she asked. 'Any idea when you're coming in? The kids are all waiting for you so they can open their presents.'

I'd become so one-track-minded, I'd forgotten about Santa Claus and turkey and mince pies. It was a reality check. Horses are wonderful, but so are my family and it was time to find a balance between the two again.

Chapter 4

Lucy and Freddy

At around the time Greatwood became a charity in 1998, the British Racing Industry was coming to accept that it had a responsibility to put a fund in place for retired or neglected racehorses. Only around 300 of the 4,000 to 5,000 racehorses retired annually need charitable intervention, but looking after 300 Thoroughbreds a year is an expensive and labour-intensive job by anyone's standards.

More and more stories were appearing in the press and the momentum for change was building. Carrie Humble, founder of the Thoroughbred Rehabilitation Centre in Lancashire, together with Vivien McIrvine, Vice President of the International League for the Protection of Horses, and Graham Oldfield and Sue Collins, founders of Moorcroft Racing Welfare Centre, formed part of a well-established racing group and were all influential in the decision that racing should try to help those ex-racehorses that had fallen upon hard times.

In January 1999 the British Horseracing Board Retired Racing Welfare Group was set up, chaired by Brigadier Andrew Parker Bowles, and the first meeting was held at Portman Square in London. It was quite an effort for Michael and me to get there. We lived at least an hour's drive away from Exeter station, and from there it was the best part of three hours' train journey to London, which meant we had to head off straight after the morning feed, long before the sun was up, but it was important that we attended come what may.

The debate was lively, to say the least. One old gent told me that in his opinion the best thing to do with ex-racehorses was shoot them. Eventually, though, a consensus was reached. Everyone at the meeting – including leading representatives from all areas of horseracing – agreed that set-ups such as ours were a vital safety net for the racing profession. In recognition of this, it was agreed that the Industry would put in place a fund to provide annual grants to accredited establishments, and Greatwood was to be one of them.

So far so good, but the details were not discussed and we didn't know when the funding would start or how it would be administered. It was gratifying that our collective voices had at least been heard, but we were still flat out to the boards caring for the horses that were currently in our care and keeping an eye on those that we had rehomed. So in short, yes, we were pleased that our work was at last recognised but, more to the point, when would this support be forthcoming?

Our local paper started a campaign and it was picked up by some of the national media, thus helping to raise our profile, but we continued to live on a knife edge. Each horse cost £100 a week to keep and we had more than twenty in our care at any one time, which meant £2000 a week or £104,000 a year. We were so short of money that we were always just a hair's breadth away from our overdraft limit and robbing Peter to pay Paul on a weekly basis. We stretched our credit cards to the maximum, but they wouldn't quite cover the ongoing expenses.

During that time of great anxiety, we really valued our friendship with Father Jeremy and his wife Clarissa. She often brought groups of children to the farm to visit, and she would supply sumptuous picnics that we could all enjoy: cakes with flamboyant coloured icing topped with seasonal decorations, sausages, sandwiches, buns and home-made biscuits. There was always far too much and the leftovers would feed Michael and me for a couple of days afterwards. I suspect she planned it that way.

The horses never seemed to mind little people rushing around whooping and shrieking. Even the most nervous mares that were startled by cars would lower their heads to allow the children to stroke their noses, turning a blind eye to the general mayhem. For their part the children begged to be allowed to ride a horse and, after some consideration, we nominated Chic as the calmest, steadiest one.

Chic was still looking after Jack, her adoptive foal, but she was happy to let the children sit on her back and was careful not to move a muscle when they clustered around her feet. Whenever I climbed on her, she tended to fidget but with the kids she stood stock still. She looked after them just as well as she looked after Jack, always keeping an eye out for him no matter what else was going on.

One day I photographed Chic with several children on her back and sent a copy of the picture to Vivien McIrvine, along with another photo of a group of kids who had climbed a haystack and were jumping off with unfurled umbrellas in an attempt to imitate Mary Poppins. I'd wanted her to see how well it was all going, but the very next day the phone rang.

'Helen, what on earth do you think you are doing? Do you have any idea of the litigation that would follow if one of those kids falls and injures himself? If there's an accident, you'd all be for the high jump!'

It shows how naïve I was back then that the possibility hadn't even occurred to me. I thought it was great that everyone was having such a lovely time and never considered any repercussions. After that I made sure the children always wore hard hats before riding the horses, but I still let them mess around and let off steam. It had to be exciting on the farm or they wouldn't have wanted to come.

The children came in groups of twelve to fifteen at a time, and it wasn't all fun and games for them, because I set them to work mucking out, helping with the feeding or sweeping the yard. They didn't seem to mind because the same few came back time after time, dropped off and picked up by their parents. One Saturday, we got a phone call from a man we knew through the church.

'I've heard you have children coming to the farm to help, and I wondered if we could bring my daughter Lucy?' he asked.

'Of course,' I said straight away, then added quickly, 'What age is she?' I didn't want to end up babysitting for someone I'd have to take to the loo all the time.

'Fourteen.'

'That's fine, then.'

He hesitated. 'It's just that … Lucy's been having a bit of trouble at school. I don't know exactly what's going on but she doesn't seem to have any friends and she's unhappy. We have to drag her out the door in the morning. I thought maybe she could make some new friends at Greatwood, and be of use to you at the same time.'

My curiosity was aroused. 'Of course she can come. I look forward to meeting her.'

An hour later, a car pulled into the yard and our friend got out along with a lanky girl with a shock of ginger hair. Her legs were so skinny her kneecaps looked like hubcaps, and when she smiled I saw her teeth were too big for her mouth. She was at an awkward age.

'Hi, Lucy,' I said, shaking her hand. 'There are some other kids mucking out in that barn over there. If you'd like to join them, someone will find you a shovel.' I didn't believe in hanging around exchanging pleasantries while there was work to be done. 'Don't worry – I'll keep an eye on her,' I promised her dad before he drove off.

I left the children in the barn on their own for a bit, then curiosity got the better of me and I sneaked up to listen in to the conversation I could hear in snatches.

'I know all about horses,' I heard Lucy saying. 'I've been riding since I was about two years old.'

'No one can ride at two,' another kid intervened.

'Well, I did,' Lucy said. 'I've ridden lots of racehorses. There's not a horse I can't ride. My dad's going to buy me a horse of my own soon. Maybe he'll get one of the ones here.'

Her dad hadn't mentioned any such thing to me and I knew they didn't have the space or the money to keep a horse, but maybe there was some kind of misunderstanding.

Later that morning, Chic was in the yard and I decided to offer Lucy a chance to ride her. 'Lucy, I overheard you saying you like riding. Would you like to have a go on Chic?'

She blushed and mumbled something to the ground and I assumed she felt shy with me, and perhaps embarrassed that I had overheard her boasting.

'She's out in the yard here. Come along.'

At 15.3, Chic is quite a big horse for a smallish girl. I wouldn't have let Lucy ride off on her but planned to lead her round the yard on Chic's back. But as soon as I legged her up, I realised she didn't have a clue what to do because she nearly fell straight off the other side. I looked up at her face and saw that she was ashen. She was utterly terrified. I don't think she'd ever been on a horse before and suddenly there she was, more than five feet off the ground, having told everyone she was an experienced rider. The other children were all standing around watching so I knew I had to find a way to get her off without making her lose face.

'Goodness, silly me,' I exclaimed. 'I haven't got any stirrups short enough for you. I'm sorry but you won't be able to ride today after all. Do you want to come down?'

I caught her as she slid off Chic's back and skulked back into the barn again.

Later I told Michael about it. 'I bet that's why she hasn't got friends at school if she's always boasting and making up stories. Why do you think she feels the need to do that?'

'They're a good, loving family. I suppose she just feels insecure for some reason. Are you happy to have her come back and help again?'

'Of course, yes. The more the merrier. It might be good for her.'

I kept half an eye out for Lucy from then on and I realised she wasn't stupid – in fact she seemed rather bright – but she was so eager to be liked that she overdid

it. If she went up to cuddle a dog, she clung on so hard
that it wriggled away yelping. When she approached a
hen to catch it, she was too keen and scared it off. She
tried her hardest to make friends with the other children,
but she did everything the wrong way. If she wasn't boasting that her dad was loaded, or that she could read a book
faster than anyone else, or that she was top of the class,
then she was laughing raucously at her own, unfunny
jokes. The other children soon began to give her a wide
berth, and I didn't blame them, but the more they tried to
avoid her, the harder Lucy tried to make them like her.

I had a groom at the time called Sandy who helped us to
train the horses. She was about twenty and Lucy was desperate to get on with her. She was cloying in her affections but
still she used completely the wrong tactics. Instead of listening to Sandy's conversation, Lucy felt she had to impress her
with her knowledge of pop music, or computers, or things
that were all far too old for her. Whatever Sandy said, she
had to go one better. If Sandy had a new CD, Lucy boasted
that she had seen the band live in concert. If Sandy
mentioned a TV programme she liked, Lucy claimed to
have it on video. Sandy was kind to her, but I could tell Lucy
annoyed her with her constant wheedling. I knew that
inside she was a frightened little girl, but I had no idea how
to teach that girl better social skills. Where do you start?

Despite her lack of friends at Greatwood, Lucy was
obviously happy with us. One Saturday, her father got out
of the car and came over to have a word.

'Lucy's mother and I are so grateful for everything you're doing for her,' he said. 'The school holidays are just starting and we wondered if she could spend more time here. Only if she's useful, of course.'

In fact, she was a good worker, picking things up the first time she was told, and thinking for herself if need be. 'I'd be delighted,' I said.

'I think she might be interested in working with horses when she leaves school, and we want to encourage her in her ambitions.'

'She should stay here for a couple of weeks and get a taste of the early starts before she makes up her mind about working with horses,' I quipped, and before I knew it, it had been agreed that Lucy would move in with us for two weeks over the summer. She'd got under my skin and I wanted to help her out if I could.

For two weeks Lucy slept in our spare room, ate her meals with us, and I didn't for one moment regret the decision. She used to get up with me at 5am to boil the huge vats of barley on our Aga for horse feed. She'd help feed the other animals as well, then wash out the feed buckets, muck out the barns, and keep everything neat and tidy around the yard. She became adept at slipping a head collar on the horses and talking quietly to them when they needed to stand still, for example if the farrier was there to trim their hooves. All in all, she was a great asset to me – but still the other children didn't warm to her.

While Lucy was there, we had a visit one day from a racehorse owner driving a Mercedes, who'd come to check us out and decide if we were the best home for one of his retired horses. I think the stables were a lot more dilapidated than he was used to, but when he saw the condition of our animals, he agreed that his horse, Freddy, could come to us. He duly arrived the next day in a smart trailer. Freddy was a smallish bay with a white blaze down his nose and he was in peak condition, having only come out of training a few weeks before. He danced about as he was unloaded, putting flight to the hens and some geese.

Freddy had had an ignominious end to his ten-year racing career, going from being the winner of Group 1 races at the age of two to trailing at the back of the field more recently. It would take a degree of expertise to retrain him for another career, but I thought we had a good chance of managing it. I stood him in a stable for a day or so to get used to us, then Lucy was with me when I led him up to the field at the end of the lane where we kept our other geldings. Freddy was as naughty as a two-year-old colt, rearing up on his hind legs as I led him, and I thought, 'Uh-oh, we're going to have our work cut out.' He was obviously a highly strung creature.

As soon as I released him into the field, he galloped straight up to the other horses and tried to push his way into the middle of the herd. He obviously didn't know that there was a pecking order in a herd and new members have to approach slowly and show respect. One horse nosed him roughly out of the way, then another did the same.

'What are they doing?' Lucy cried, and I realised she had tears in her eyes. 'They're going to hurt him.'

'No, they won't,' I said, watching carefully just in case I was wrong. Freddy approached the group again, but they wouldn't let him near, rejecting his advances until eventually, head down, he wandered off to graze on his own in a corner.

'Why won't they be friends with him?' Lucy asked, her voice cracking.

Suddenly I realised this was touching a raw nerve for her and I chose my words carefully. 'Freddy's been used to being on his own a lot, or with his trainer and jockey, and he's forgotten how to get on with other horses. He has to earn his place in the herd and wait for them to invite him in instead of charging full pelt into the middle and demanding attention. But don't worry. It will work itself out eventually.'

'He must be really upset about it.'

'Yes, he probably is. But it will be all right in the end.' At least I hoped it would.

We had to supplement Freddy's diet while he adjusted to grazing, having previously been fed on concentrates. It became Lucy's job to go up to the field twice a day and feed him from a bucket, trying to keep it hidden from the rest of the herd so they didn't think he was getting special treatment, which would have made things much harder.

As Lucy fed him, she would stroke his nose and whisper to him, and it was obvious that this lonely girl felt a great affinity for the lonely horse.

From time to time, if another horse was standing separately from the rest of the herd, Freddy would try another approach, sauntering up hopefully, but he was usually met with a hostile kick or a push. He'd panic then canter away again to his solitary grazing. After a few days of this, he started to get nervous when other horses came near and I was concerned that the situation wasn't resolving itself as quickly as I'd hoped. Fear is always alienating. If a child is scared of dogs and starts behaving oddly around them, even the friendliest breeds of dog will respond by barking or jumping up and will scare the child even more. However, if a child can stay calm, the dogs will be calm too, and it's the same with horses. Freddy would have to learn to calm down, and this would take time.

'Why don't they understand that he only wants to make friends?' Lucy asked me over and over again.

'He's already got a friend,' I told her. 'Have you noticed how much he brightens up when you come along?' It was true. Freddy always rushed over as soon as he saw Lucy approaching the field, whether she was carrying a feed bucket or not. One day, I saw the two of them lying on the grass beside each other, with Lucy chatting quietly and Freddy still and listening. I would have loved to have eavesdropped but if they'd noticed me, it would have spoiled the moment.

'Freddy was lying down in the field today,' Lucy told me later, and I knew that was a good sign, because it meant he was settling and wasn't so scared of the others.

Not long after that, there were a few telltale signs that Freddy was being accepted by the herd. It started with some sniffing of noses, and then a little grooming of necks. Freddy let the others make the approach without either running away or responding with too much eagerness, and in return it seemed they were beginning to accept him.

Around this time, I watched Lucy trying to catch Flirty Gertie one morning, trying hard not to laugh as she kept slipping out of reach. Finally I stepped in to help. I talked to Gertie quietly, approaching very gradually then stooping down using slow, careful movements, and she let me pick her up.

'Do you see how I did that?' I asked. 'You can't force your presence on a hen, especially not one like Gertie. You need to gain her trust first of all.'

'OK,' Lucy nodded, and over the next few days I watched her get the hang of it. She was getting on better with the dogs as well, and one lunchtime I eavesdropped while Sandy was telling her about a new CD she'd bought and Lucy didn't interrupt once to boast that she had better CDs at home. She was learning.

I'd like to say Lucy became friends with the other children at Greatwood that summer, but nothing happens that quickly after a bad first impression has been formed.

However, she made a firm friend of Freddy. After the two weeks she stayed with us, Lucy kept popping back to see Freddy whenever she could, and as soon as he spotted her coming down the lane, Freddy would rush up to the fence to greet her. There was a meeting of kindred spirits there that I think helped both of them through a difficult time.

The summer holidays ended and Lucy went back to school, so she could only visit us at weekends. Her father phoned us one evening, though.

'I can't thank you enough for what you did for Lucy over the summer,' he said. 'She seems much more settled at school and has made some new friends, so we're very grateful.'

'So are we,' I said. 'She helped us to settle a highly temperamental racehorse who needed the kind of one-to-one attention I didn't have time to give it. Your daughter is good with horses. She has a knack.'

A few months later, Lucy's family moved overseas and we lost touch. Still, we felt something rather wonderful had happened. We were feeling particularly pleased with ourselves when we got a sharp reminder not to take anything for granted – the bank foreclosed our account. We couldn't take out cash or write cheques for anything any more. In order to keep going, we had to sit down and apply for as many credit cards as we could, with the maximum credit limit they would give us. From now on we would be living off the never-never.

Chapter 5

Sophie and Darcy Day

A car pulling a trailer came up the drive and stopped in the yard one morning in late summer. Usually horses start stamping when their trailer comes to a standstill but there was no sound from this one and I worried that its occupant might have got injured on the journey, and might even be down, although I would have thought that the driver would have heard if anything untoward had happened.

Michael let the tailgate down and a desperate sight met my eyes. Darcy was bony, her head hanging low over the bars, and her coat was matted and discoloured. Over the years, I'd seen many horses in poor condition but this one rocked me on my heels. I climbed into the trailer to untie her, talking in a soft, low voice, but she didn't even raise her head to look at me. This was an animal who had given up on the world.

The woman driver introduced herself and told us that she had rescued Darcy from a place where she was being severely neglected but that she couldn't afford to keep her herself. Would we be able to help? Of course we would. There was no question. I was just concerned about how I was going to get her to back down the ramp out of the trailer because she was in such weak condition she could have collapsed at any time.

Gently, step by faltering step, Michael guided her down while I helped at the other end, until she stood trembling in the yard in front of us. She was a mess. Her eyes were dull and streaming, her bones protruding through her coat, her hind legs swollen and oozing a yellow discharge, her tail a tangled mass of wet hair and diarrhoea, her hooves long and overgrown. Her temperature was sky high and I knew she needed intravenous medication quickly. I went indoors to ring Adrian, the local vet, while Michael led Darcy slowly to the old sheep barn where she could be nursed in peace. We had a nursery paddock in front of the house where we sometimes put poorly horses because we could listen out for them in the night, but it was clear that Darcy was nowhere near well enough to be outside.

When Adrian arrived, he whistled through his teeth. The strain of the journey had obviously taken its toll on Darcy. She was clearly very distressed and had broken out in a heavy sweat. Her temperature remained way above normal, her hind legs were hot and swollen and the skin had split in several places.

'It's a nasty case of lymphangitis,' Adrian said, 'started from infected cuts on her legs.' He injected her with a hefty dose of painkillers, as well as antibiotics and anti-inflammatories to kick-start the healing process.

Michael brought out some buckets of warm water and Adrian cleaned Darcy's hind legs as best he could, then bandaged them. He bathed her eyes and put in some eyedrops. The only good news to emerge from his head-to-hoof medical check was that she didn't have lice, which would have meant that we would have been forced to keep her in isolation.

'She may develop colic,' Adrian said. 'I can't tell yet. You'll have to keep a close eye on her temperature and watch her like a hawk for the next few days to see if she turns the corner.'

The word 'if' hung in the air. What he was saying was that there was a good chance she wouldn't. This horse seemed to have lost the will to live.

'She needs company,' I said to Michael. 'Maybe if we bring in another horse and they get along together, she'll perk up a bit.'

He agreed – but which one should it be?

'Tish!' we both said together.

Tish was a little Shetland pony, only 28 inches tall, who had come to us after a horrific incident in which several men had attacked him with shovels and beaten him badly, all because he bit a child who was petting him at a show. Who knows what that child was actually doing to him at the time? Those men didn't wait to hear if there had been any provocation before laying into him. Once he arrived at Greatwood and recovered from his beating, we found Tish to be a cheeky, cheerful, entertaining character with a strong personality, who wouldn't let any of the much bigger horses take advantage. He'd be the ideal equine companion for Darcy: too small to appear a threat, but perky enough to attract her attention.

I went out to the field to try to catch Tish – no mean feat when he doesn't want to be caught – and finally managed to lead him to the sheep barn where Darcy was standing alone in the corner. Tish marched straight in and helped himself to a huge mouthful of the fresh meadow hay we had left for Darcy. Darcy looked up, surprised, then edged over to sniff Tish's bottom. Tish gave a swift warning kick with one of his back feet and carried on munching. Darcy went over to stand beside him, avoiding the back legs, looked cautiously out of the corner of her eye, and then bent down and picked up a wisp of hay in her mouth. They stood side by side eating from the same pile, which meant they were accepting each other. It was a huge step forwards for Darcy.

For the rest of the day Tish and Darcy ignored each other but at the same time continued to be quite happy in each other's company, so we felt confident enough to leave them overnight in the same barn. Next morning, I hurried outside as soon as I awoke to find Darcy's temperature had gone down. Her eyes were brightening and she was obviously feeling a lot better, although she still paid no attention to Michael or me. She accepted everything we did for her with a resigned air but without any responsiveness or gratitude.

We had to walk her a few times a day to help the swelling in her legs, and when we led her out of the barn, Tish would call out for her and she would whinny in reply. A relationship was forming. Within three days, they were inseparable and when we wanted to take Darcy out for a walk, Tish had to be taken along as well. Darcy had made a friend.

A few days after Darcy's arrival, a car pulled into the yard and a woman wound down the window to talk to Michael.

'We heard that you have children here to help on Saturday mornings and we wondered if you would have our daughter Sophie?'

He glanced into the back seat and saw a dark-haired girl staring at her lap. 'OK,' he said. 'That's fine.'

The woman started talking, and it was as if the floodgates opened. 'Her father and I are very worried. You see, she's stopped talking – she hasn't spoken a word for two years. We don't know what to do but she likes reading books about horses and we heard about you and thought maybe …'

'That's fine,' Michael said again, curious now about this girl who seemingly didn't talk.

'We'll be back in a couple of hours,' the mother said. 'We don't want her to be a burden to you. We'll just do a bit of shopping and come back. She's got a mobile phone in her pocket with our number on it and if she rings, we'll come straight away.'

The car door opened and Sophie stepped out, a sullen look on her face. She was overweight and had made no effort with her appearance, with her baggy, ill-fitting clothes and her lanky, unwashed hair. But more than that, it was her general demeanour that told me she was depressed. She was hunched, as though there were a heavy weight pressing down on her, and she could barely find the energy to lift one foot after the other and walk.

As her parents drove off, I swept over and introduced myself. 'I'm just on the way to change the dressings on a horse called Darcy,' I told her. 'Come with me.' On the way to the barn, I explained about the condition Darcy had arrived in just a few days earlier and what steps we were taking to try to help her. There was no reaction and I began to wonder if Sophie had a hearing as well as a speech problem.

And then the three of us – Michael, Sophie and me – walked into the barn, and Darcy astonished us by going straight over to Sophie and lowering her head to be petted.

'I brought her a great big breakfast this morning and she never comes over to me,' I complained, but really I didn't mind at all. We never ask for anything in return from horses we rescue. That's not how it works.

I could tell Sophie was pleased. She held out her hands and Darcy put her nose into them. Even though she must still have been feeling rotten with her legs and all her other health complaints, she was able to make a connection with this silent little child.

I laid out the equipment for changing the dressings and as I worked, I asked Sophie to hand me the items I needed. She seemed bright enough, finding the correct bandages or tubes of ointment and holding them out until I was ready to take them, but it felt strange talking to someone who never talked back. Michael and I found ourselves chatting more than we normally would have just to fill the silence.

After I'd finished with Darcy, I led Sophie to the hen house and showed her how to look for eggs, and how to feed the chickens, then she just trailed round helping me with my normal jobs for the next couple of hours until her parents came back. I decided not to introduce her to the rest of the children in the stable, because they wouldn't have been able to resist asking questions and possibly even making fun of her. It seemed better to keep her busy and out of the way of the others.

When Sophie saw her parents' car, she walked across to it with the same sullen posture as when she'd arrived, opened the back door and climbed in. She didn't so much as wave goodbye to us.

'Thank you very much,' her mother shouted out of the window as they left.

'Do you think she'll be back next week?' I asked Michael.

'I don't know.'

'She seems very troubled. I wonder what that could be about?'

'Who knows? Perhaps she's perfectly capable of speaking and has just decided to rebel, but you'd think the odd word would have slipped out at some stage over the last two years.' Michael rubbed his chin thoughtfully.

'I was wondering if she's had some kind of traumatic experience. Maybe she's being bullied at school.'

I'd been bullied myself, back at the age of thirteen. We'd left the farm where I'd had such a happy childhood with my horses, and moved to a town. At the new school I was sent to, the other girls found me very unstreetwise. They were interested in boys and dating, while all I cared about was animals. On the first day, one girl ran a finger down my back to see if I was wearing a bra, and they all laughed when they found I wasn't. They weren't violent towards me but they treated me as though I were some lowly creature, not worthy of attention, so I've always felt sympathetic to any children in the same situation.

During the following week, my thoughts kept returning to Sophie and I wondered whether I should have handled her differently, but I decided that my policy of just treating her as if everything were completely normal was the best one. She didn't want me bombarding her with questions and I'm sure she'd had enough people coaxing and cajoling her to speak both at home and at school. It seemed most natural to me to pretend everything was fine, that her silence was nothing out of the ordinary.

The following Saturday, I was surprised but pleased when I saw her parents' car pulling into the yard and watched Sophie climbing out of the back door.

'Is it all right if she stays another couple of hours with you this morning?' her mother called.

'Yes, of course,' I replied. 'Sophie, do you want to come and see Darcy? Her legs are much better than they were last week.'

She followed me eagerly, and once again Darcy came over to see her as soon as we entered the barn, making a gentle whickering sound. She definitely recognised Sophie, because she didn't get up and come over to any of the other children. I told Sophie this and she looked very pleased.

'Why don't I teach you how to groom her?' I suggested. 'These are the brushes here.' I showed her how to stand round the back of the horse and start by feeling it all over with your hands, smoothing down in the direction of the hair, watching the horse's reaction to your touch, before you start work with a brush. I told her that the tummy can be tickly so you've got to apply the right amount of pressure, and cautioned her to avoid Darcy's injured legs.

Sophie started work with enthusiasm, concentrating hard on doing the job to the best of her ability. Darcy was enjoying it so much that her eyelids began to droop and she almost nodded off on her feet. That's a huge compliment from a horse, implying absolute trust, and it was yet another sign of the growing bond between them.

I took the opportunity to go and have a chat with the other children who were there that day. I explained to them about Sophie not talking and asked them just to treat her normally and not to refer to it. Bless them, they were as good as gold, accepting her as one of the crowd and ignoring the fact that she never joined in their conversations.

At the end of the morning, when the work was finished and the kids were waiting for their parents to pick them up, I usually invited them into the kitchen for a drink. I remember thinking on that second Saturday that Sophie seemed much more animated than before. Her eyes were sparkling, and when I asked if she would like a Coke, she nodded and smiled her thanks at me.

'She seems happy enough here,' Michael commented later. 'I hope it does her some good.'

It felt odd at first that you talked to someone and there was no response, but we soon got used to it and hardly gave it a second thought. Sophie got into a routine of coming every Saturday and as soon as she got out of the car, she'd run to Darcy's stable to see her. She slipped into the rhythm of the work on the farm, did as she was told, laughed and smiled with the other children, and seemed the same as them – until you stopped and realised that she was just listening rather than joining in their conversations.

Meanwhile, Darcy continued to recover. Her legs healed, her coat improved and she started to take an interest in life. Every Saturday Sophie would groom her until she was gleaming, and when I took her out for a walk around the yard, Sophie would come along, walking proudly by her side. She obviously felt possessive because whenever she could, she would slip into Darcy's stable and sit on a bank of straw, just watching. Tish would stride around grumpily and I often heard her laughing at him. It was a pretty laugh, and it made me curious to hear her speaking voice.

There were a couple of occasions when I could feel that Sophie wanted to say something to me. Once I dropped Darcy's bundle of hay on one side of the barn and Sophie made a noise that sounded like mild protest.

'What is it?' I asked.

She looked at me for a moment then rose, picked up the hay and moved it to the other side, and I remembered that that was where Darcy seemed to prefer it. It's hard to remember every single horse's individual preferences when you are feeding twenty of them every day, but Sophie knew exactly what Darcy liked.

'I think she wants to talk,' I told Michael later, 'but I'm not sure if she can. Maybe there's a physical problem?'

'Her parents told me they'd explored every avenue,' he said, 'and I'm sure that's true. I can sympathise with her, but I can also imagine her parents' frustration as the weeks and months went by without her saying a word.

They must want to grab her and shout "For goodness' sake, will you just speak?"'

On a few other occasions, I heard Sophie make sounds that were like speech when she wanted to tell me something about Darcy, but they never came out as fully formed words. We got used to her muteness. It's just the way she was. We were delighted to see her looking happier and more relaxed than when she first came to us, and we didn't ask for anything more. When her parents' car drew into the yard, she'd leap out, wave gaily at us and rush straight to Darcy's barn to say hello. She'd smile and laugh, and enter into any fun going on in the yard, such as when the kids were splashing each other with water. She was a changed girl in many ways.

Towards the end of the summer, the volunteers were in the kitchen having their drinks while waiting for their parents. Michael and I were having a cup of tea and chatting to each other. Sophie was just round the corner from where we were standing. Suddenly Michael put his finger to his lips, then pointed to his ear, indicating that I should listen to something.

A girl's voice was speaking. 'I was just walking across the yard,' it said, 'which is a long way from the stable, but Darcy knew straight away I was there and she started to whinny. She always knows when I'm coming.'

I frowned and mouthed the word 'Sophie?' to Michael, and he nodded. We were both amazed. Her voice was childish-sounding but perfectly clear. I couldn't work out who she was speaking to, so I wandered out casually, picking up an empty glass from the table, and glanced round at her to see she had her mobile phone to her ear.

I walked back to Michael and whispered, 'She's phoning someone.'

Soon after that, her parents' car pulled up outside. As she ran out to it, I called from the doorway, 'Bye, Sophie. See you next week!' and to my astonishment she called back, 'Bye!'

Her mother phoned me during the week. 'What on earth did you do?' she asked. 'She's talking again completely normally, as if she had never stopped.'

'We didn't do anything …'

When Michael and I discussed it later, he said, 'It's about confidence. Something must have happened to Sophie two years ago that made her lose her confidence. Through her relationship with Darcy, she got it back again. Horses are powerful therapy.'

Secretly, I wondered if she had been talking to one or two friends all along and it was just with adults that she was silent? I never found out.

By the end of summer, Darcy was healthy enough to go out into a field with the other horses. First of all we tentatively let her out into a field with Tish, then as she got stronger, we introduced her to the other mares, and all went well. It meant that her close one-to-one relationship with Sophie changed, but she still cantered over to the fence whenever she saw Sophie nearby. Her eyes were bright and shiny, her coat glossy and there was no remaining sign of the poorly creature who had arrived in a trailer just a few weeks earlier.

Once she had started talking, Sophie never stopped. She chattered all day long about the horses, and became quite bossy with other children who hadn't been coming to the farm as long as she had.

'You don't hold the brush like that,' I overheard her saying as she supervised the grooming one day. 'Do this.' She demonstrated with perfect technique.

I never asked her why she hadn't spoken for so long, never commented on the fact that she had started speaking again. I felt it wasn't my business. I was just glad if coming to Greatwood had been the catalyst for her to get back to being a normal teenager again.

It gave Michael an idea, though. We knew of a couple of organisations that used horses to help adults with mental health issues. It seemed that they found fresh ways to look at life through their communication with animals, and many people turned the corner as a result. We didn't have any experience of working with people with mental health issues, but we wondered if we could offer the same kind of experience that Sophie had on the farm. Children with problems could come along, get involved and see what they made of it.

The germ of a plan was born, but before we could take it any further, we had a string of tragedies to cope with, one after another.

Chapter 6

Moving to Wiltshire

Chic had been one of our steadiest, most attractive horses, with her liver chestnut colouring and her child-friendly, easy-going nature. She'd always been an attentive mother to the orphan foal Jack, but after he was weaned and left Greatwood, Chic started to look off colour. It was nothing I could put my finger on but she had definitely lost her spark. The inside of her mouth was pale and dry so I called Adrian, the vet, who did some blood tests and gave her a vitamin injection to try to perk her up.

Over the next few weeks Chic deteriorated steadily, and Adrian began to suspect she had an auto-immune disease of some kind. She spent a week at the vet's while he administered a cocktail of drugs, trying to find the right balance, then she came back for us to look after her at home, but all the while she was weakening. She was getting tired of all the injections, yet she couldn't manage without the drugs. When we tried taking her off them, she went downhill rapidly.

I cried every time I left her stable. I couldn't help myself. She was only twelve years old, while most horses can expect to live to at least twenty. It wasn't fair, but we knew she was suffering and finally we had to make the decision to put her to sleep. I held her head as she was given the fatal injection and my heart was breaking. I'd done this before, of course, but instead of getting easier it seemed to get harder every time.

Chic left a big hole in our lives. She'd been the sensible, dependable one of the bunch. Nothing ever fazed her. Michael and I referred to her as 'Dot Cotton' after the *EastEnders* character who often stands around with a ciggie in her mouth commenting wryly on events in the Square. I missed her badly, and several of the other horses did as well. Tish in particular was inconsolable for weeks.

Shortly after this, Jelly, the bolshy grey that used to barge me whenever I entered her stable, fell ill. She had melanomas in her throat that were growing larger, she'd lost a lot of weight and we had no choice but to put her down as well. We buried her next to Chic and I shed genuine tears. Although we hadn't started out as the best of friends, Jelly had been a strong character, a steady horse that had been a distinctive presence on the farm.

Poppy, the very first horse we had taken on many moons earlier, was a huge comfort to me during this period. Despite her early feistiness, she had grown into the kindest and gentlest of mares and I came to love her more than I have ever loved any other horse. She reminded me of Shadow, the horse I'd ridden when I was a child. They had the same colouring and the same way of looking at me as if they understood everything I was saying. Whenever I felt upset I'd go and sit with Poppy in her stable and she'd lower her head to nibble at my hair. Sometimes we'd ride out down the valley, jumping over fences and leaping puddles, and she was so instinctive that she knew what I wanted her to do almost before I knew myself. Riding out with her never failed to lift my spirits.

Poppy became my helper round the farm. I'd ride her round the fields to check on the other horses and she stood rock-still when I had to leap off to fasten gates or examine a particular horse. She seemed to sense that this was her job. When I had to bring the other nineteen horses in on my own, I would lead the first horse while she brought up the rear, and she could be relied upon to usher in any malingerer that had stopped for a nibble at the verge. She'd wait patiently as I put each horse in its stable, and saw to her last. She was behaving like a stallion, or the leading mare at least, and her help was invaluable to me.

Bleak times came for the whole countryside with the February 2001 foot and mouth outbreak. We had to stop all visitors coming to Greatwood, and we couldn't ride outside the farm. Most of our neighbours' flocks of sheep were culled and the sky was dark with the smoke from countless bonfires of carcasses. One day I thought the sky was full of tiny white petals, until I realised that the wind was carrying ash from the animal bonfires. It settled eerily on the surface of water troughs, and on the backs of the horses.

We had a visit from the white-overalled men from the Ministry of Agriculture, Forestry and Fisheries, who took blood samples from our two remaining sheep and Angie and Monty, the goats. It was nerve-racking waiting for the results but fortunately, by some miracle, they were all fine. Thank goodness we'd got rid of the rest of our sheep when we did. It was awful for our neighbours, though, and we saw many grown men reduced to tears as they watched their sheep being killed one by one, and their livelihood going up in smoke.

Once the outbreak had passed and we were allowed to have visitors again, Michael made an appointment with Devon County Education Authority to ask if there was any interest in us starting a scheme whereby children with special needs could come and work with our race-horses. He told them about our experience with Sophie and Darcy, and to our astonishment they agreed straight away. We'd been expecting loads of bureaucratic hurdles but they were all in favour of the scheme and offered to put us in touch with some of the local special schools. As soon as we contacted them, they all replied that they would love to send over some kids. They'd come with their own teachers and supervisors, so we didn't need any special qualifications ourselves. Everyone we spoke to seemed very excited about the whole idea.

We realised we'd need some kind of reception area where we could talk to the children about what happened at Greatwood and warn them about health and safety issues before leading them out to the stables. They'd also need loos they could use, wash basins to wash their hands after touching the animals, and possibly somewhere to sit down with a packed lunch. We had a derelict outbuilding at the top of the drive and we reckoned it would make an ideal reception area. We thought we could raise the money needed for the conversion from a couple of local children's charities. So far, so good.

Then a major spoke appeared in the works. We applied to our landlords for permission to convert the outbuilding, thinking it would just be a formality, but not only did they refuse our request, they also said that they didn't want us to have children visiting the farm any more. They said it wouldn't work because of their pheasant-shooting business, as it was too risky to have children running around.

It was a huge blow, and we tried to challenge it, but we were tenants and there was only so much we could do. We'd had an uneasy relationship with our landlords over the years. The pheasant shooting had been a problem for us because the keepers sometimes forgot to give us notice and began shooting while the horses were still in the fields, which panicked them. They used to lay a trail of wheat for the pheasants to follow and some of it blew down into our fields, which was a huge worry because even a small amount of wheat is toxic for horses. Fasci and an elderly horse called Fred had both succumbed to a nasty disease called laminitis from eating wheat, and while Fasci survived, Fred had to be put down.

Furthermore, we had a visit from the chairman of the Rehabilitation of Racehorses Trust, from whom we were hoping to get a grant. He was impressed by the condition of the horses, but felt it wasn't appropriate to give us funding while we were at our present farm due to the 'inadequacy of the facilities': it wasn't smart, we didn't have an outdoor school for training our horses and we were miles from anywhere.

Taking everything into consideration, there was no doubt that it was time to leave Greatwood. We knew it in our heart of hearts, but couldn't quite face it because the scale of the removal operation was daunting. And where would we find anywhere else with the right amount of land, outbuildings and a cottage for us to live in as well, but all for a rent we could afford? It wasn't going to be easy.

Michael began to scour the newspapers searching for suitable alternative premises. Whenever he spotted somewhere that might fit the bill, he jumped into our rusty, twenty-year-old car and set off to view it, inevitably returning later with his face betraying his disappointment. There were problems with all of the local places. He started to look further and further afield, setting off at the crack of dawn and returning late in the evening, but still nothing came up. Some farms were set right on a main road, which wouldn't work for us because the traffic noise would disturb the more nervous animals. We needed around 50 acres of land, but we didn't have a huge budget. More specifically, we needed a paddock right outside the house where we could keep vulnerable horses within earshot at night, and plenty of outbuildings that could be turned into stables. Our shopping list of demands was going to be extremely difficult to meet.

Michael spent months looking and we struggled to afford the petrol for all these trips. The car was getting more and more ropey. It was prone to over-heating and he could never go anywhere without a bottle of water for when the water tank boiled over and steam began to pour out. And the only way to open the bonnet was by using a broom handle, so he had to take one of them along as well. Everything mounted up and we were beginning to feel very gloomy indeed when an agent we knew told us about a farm up for lease near Marlborough in Wiltshire. Michael drove up there to view it and I waited at home with fingers crossed.

When he came back that night, he had some unexpected news. 'I put in an offer on the spot. There were forty other people coming for viewings and I didn't want to miss it because I think it's as close as we'll get.'

I was miffed that he'd made the decision without me seeing it, even if I could understand the reasons. 'It's near Marlborough? A town? Do you think the horses are going to be able to run around in a pub car park then?'

'Come and see it, Helen. I've made an appointment for tomorrow. I think it's going to work.'

When we got to Rainscombe Hill Farm the next morning, I could see the potential straight away. It had a motley collection of rundown stables within the barns, with broken drainpipes and electric cables dangling from the ceilings, but the barns at least were large and airy and we could rearrange things to our own designs. The fields would have to be reseeded but there were 13 acres in the basic farm area, plus an extra 29 we could add on, and that would be enough to start with. The cottage in which we would live was grimy and horrid, as houses can become when no one has cared for them for a very long time, but it would do after some major fumigation and industrial-scale cleaning.

It was just our luck that it was winter when we found the farm, so all the renovation work had to be done during the coldest, wettest months of the year. In fact, it seemed like one of the wettest winters in living memory, with every day dark and windy, and we scarcely ever saw the sun.

I advertised for staff and hired a couple of local people, who helped us to set up the barns: one for Toffee and Red; a separate house for the chickens and geese, with wire mesh over the top so they couldn't escape and the foxes couldn't get in; and a big open-plan stable for the mares, with separate stalls but low dividing walls so they could see each other.

Before leaving Devon, we were able to rehome six of our horses, including Darcy Day, so that meant we would only have to move ourselves, nineteen horses, five dogs, two sheep, two goats, a dozen chickens, Horrible Horace and a few other geese. Only. It took four days at the end of January 2002, during which I zigzagged up and down from Wiltshire to Devon and back again, taking more animals and furniture with me on each trip. There were dozens of mishaps: a rat infestation in the barns; lights in the cottage that inexplicably couldn't be switched off; a water tank that flooded all over my carefully packed linen; a horse that put his head through the roof of the transport lorry, and yet another that refused to get in. It was sad to say a final goodbye to our friends down there: Father Jeremy and Clarissa, Peter, the owner of Fasci, who had agreed she could come with us to Wiltshire, Adrian the vet, and all the other lovely people who had supported us. Now we'd have to create a new support group, find a new vet and new farriers, and make new friends.

Amazingly, all the animals adapted well to the move except one: Poppy, my favourite. During the last few months in Devon she had become reluctant to go out and graze in the field, and seemed happier to stand on her own in her stable. I'd been too busy to give it much thought, simply assuming that she preferred being in the dry warmth of the stable to outside in the rain. In all other respects she seemed fine. But after we moved to Wiltshire she began to panic if we tried to lead her out, and there was a danger someone could have been trampled as she barged and bolted frantically. This was completely out of character for the Poppy I knew and loved.

I'd have assumed the problem was something to do with the move, but that didn't make sense because Poppy had moved home with us twice before without any trouble. As the weeks wore on, she became more unpredictable and scared, and I realised her eyesight had deteriorated. When the vet was called, he said it was a difficult diagnosis but he could only think that she had some kind of brain tumour. I was completely devastated.

You can't be selfish when you keep animals. If they are suffering or unable to enjoy a decent quality of life, you have to let them go, but Poppy was the hardest one of all because I'd got so close to her. She was a friend, someone on my side, and a reminder of the childhood relationship I'd had with Shadow. But she was confused and terrified about what was happening to her, so I had no choice but to let the vet put her down. I talked to her quietly to try to reassure her that everything was all right and that there was really nothing to be frightened about, but inside I was in pieces.

The loss of Poppy was dreadful, and just afterwards my two elderly goats, Angie and Monty, had to be put down as well. At the age of twelve, Angie had become increasingly frail and one day she just couldn't get up. Monty was the same age and had a host of problems, which would have been exacerbated if she had been left on her own without Angie. Those three had been stalwarts in Devon, with unquestioning loyalty and affection to Michael and me, and their loss brought home the enormity of the move to Wiltshire and all we had lost. Their presence had stopped me feeling quite so homesick at first, but now it hit me in a huge, powerful wave. I missed the early days at Greatwood Farm before we were registered as a charity, when we had time to build strong relationships with each individual animal and didn't have to be quite so businesslike. Poppy, Angie and Monty had been a big part of that time and as I mourned for them, I mourned for Greatwood as well.

I wasn't the only one. Several of the animals were calling for their missing friends for days afterwards. Angie had tended to be the leader of the motley crew of sheep and goats when they went out to grass and without her they were nervous, not venturing far and running for cover at the slightest noise. It was going to be a difficult adjustment for all of us.

Chapter 7

Edward Joins the Team

As soon as the racing community realised that Greatwood had moved to Wiltshire, and that we were now much more easily accessible than we had been in the depths of rural Devon, we began to get a flood of phone calls from people asking us to take horses. Some came from the RSPCA or equine charities, while others were from trainers looking for homes for their retiring racehorses. We erected a Portakabin to accommodate a small office and reception centre for visitors and moved in all our files, a couple of desks, and a kettle to make coffee.

We weren't yet ready to pursue the idea of having children with special needs come to visit because for a long time we were living on a building site. The whole place was a tip. All the fencing was rotting and falling down. Fields were filled with old tyres that had been dumped, and there was rubbish everywhere. Before we could do anything else, fences had to be mended, stables repaired and creosoted, the large iron barn doors fixed and painted, and the dreary breeze blocks painted white.

We wanted to use the same Greatwood logo with the girl and the horse that we'd had in Devon but discussed at length what colour it should be. Red was too angry, yellow was too bright, green was used in practically every equestrian yard throughout the country, so finally we settled on the colour purple. I'd got married in purple, and it was my favourite colour. We had our purple Greatwood signs printed and erected, then printed new stationery and business cards. We even had sweatshirts made up in Greatwood purple with the logo printed on them that we could hand out to staff and volunteers. There was so much to do that we were all working flat out, all day and every day.

I was always happiest mucking around in the fields and barns looking after our horses, but a significant part of my time now had to be spent fundraising in order to subsidise the charity. We took a stand at Lambourn Open Day to try to raise money and explain to the wider equine community about the work we did. It was daunting because there must have been about fifty stands altogether, all surrounding the arena. Racing enthusiasts were invited to go round the trainers' yards in the morning and then enjoy the array of entertainments in the arena in the afternoon. Thousands of people came by our stand, and Michael and I were inundated with requests for help and information. We also collected donations totalling about £1,000, which was very welcome.

Rehabilitation of Racehorses, the charity that had turned down our funding request while we were in Devon, sent a number of representatives and trustees to visit us in the new premises and they must have liked what they saw because they gave us the wonderful news that they were awarding us an annual grant of £50,000 to carry on with our work. In addition, they would contribute £21,000 towards the £50,000 expense of moving Greatwood from Devon to Wiltshire, which had wiped us out financially. This was a massive relief. It wasn't by any means all that we needed but it would take some of the pressure off and allow us to get to sleep at night without worrying about the next rent cheque.

Rehoming racehorses was an innovative idea, and it caught the interest of the TV programme *Pet Rescue*, who sent a camera crew down for two weeks to film the horses and the animals. That brought more enquiries, as did all the open days I took our stand along to. After public appearances we were always flooded with enquiries, and we usually made a few thousand pounds through donations, so they were well worth the trouble.

We were very honoured to be invited to take two of our horses to an event called 'All the Queen's Horses', part of the Golden Jubilee celebrations, in which a thousand different horses performed in a ninety-minute show. I took two very steady horses, Pekay and Owen, the latter lent to me by Vicky Smart, a friend of mine who is the wife of a well-known trainer. We'd coached them intensively beforehand and on the day they behaved impeccably despite the six-gun salutes being fired and all the other horses charging around. It was an honour to be part of it, and it helped to raise our profile a bit more. Slowly but surely our name was becoming established in the racing world.

At the end of August 2002, we organised our own first open day at the farm, to help promote our work, and we invited back several horses we had trained and rehomed over the years. Darcy Day returned in fine form, with a gleaming coat and no sign of the health problems that had made her such a pathetic creature the day she first arrived in the back of a trailer, and several others we'd looked after over the years also came. We had a celebrity football match with a number of famous jockeys taking part, and John McCririck, aka 'Big Mac', the colourful Channel 4 racing correspondent, gave a speech, cajoling everyone to dig deep into their pockets to support us and cracking some very good jokes. I also met his wife Jenny – the woman he famously calls 'The Booby' – for the first time. She immediately took us under her wing and promised to help us as much as she could. We raised £12,000, which for us was an extraordinarily useful day's work, and we made lots of great contacts as well.

Jenny was as good as her word, and proved phenomenal in helping me to raise funds. She knows everyone in

the racing world and was always introducing me to bookies, trainers and all kinds of potential donors. I got three
or four emails from her a week with helpful suggestions:
'Why don't you contact so-and-so? Here's his personal
mobile number/email address.' If she recommended me,
I was able to get through to the right person with just one
phone call. Through these contacts Greatwood managed
to take over the sponsorship of certain key races and sell
it on to the bookies, which helped our finances and our
PR. Jenny was helping us to move into a different league.

Other major supporters in the early days were Nigel
and Penny Bunter of Barbury Castle Estate, neighbours
of ours in Wiltshire. Nigel called to ask if he could come
by for a look around to see what we were doing, and I was
happy to give him a guided tour. To my huge delight, he
told us that he would like to sponsor the leading hurdle at
the Open Meeting at Cheltenham in our name. This was
an amazingly generous thing to offer. The hurdle is a
highly prestigious race and acts as a pointer for the
Champion Hurdle at the Festival in March. The publicity
and the strengthening of our profile in being connected
to this valuable race would be immeasurable. Nigel and
Penny have continued to sponsor the Greatwood Hurdle
since 2003, during which time we have seen many fine
horses follow in the footsteps of previous winners such as
Westender and Rooster Booster. Nigel and Penny add to
this generosity by throwing open their box at Cheltenham and offering hospitality to a number of Greatwood's

supporters. That first year was the first time I had ever presented the trophies following the race, and I was extremely nervous because I worried that in my typically clumsy way I would drop the trophy or trip over my own feet. Fortunately I didn't. Over the years since then, I have presented trophies on many occasions but I am still haunted by the same anxiety every time.

During that first year in Wiltshire, we took in thirty horses altogether – some of them straightforward, easy-going animals, while others had issues to be dealt with, either physical or mental or both. Some we could train and rehome, but for others all we could do was make them comfortable, and give them happiness, security and a pain-free existence for as long as we could. Despite the occasional heartbreak, we achieved some great results and in the first year we managed to rehome as many horses as we took in.

We hadn't forgotten about our idea of helping children with special needs but we hadn't done anything about it because we were still finishing off the building work and struggling to clamber out of the black hole of debt we were in, when one day Michael took a phone call asking if a twenty-year-old man called Edward, who has Down's syndrome, could visit us.

Michael said, 'Yes, of course.' It was only when he put the phone down that he stopped to wonder what level of disability Edward might have. Neither of us had any experience of people with Down's and didn't quite know what to expect. All we were told in advance was that he lived locally in a house with three other lads, although his parents were quite close by, and that he loved horses. He'd done some riding when he was younger, and someone at the organisation Riding for the Disabled had suggested to his key worker that he might volunteer for us.

We took to Edward straight away from the very first time he was dropped off by taxi, because he had such a big, engaging smile. He was beaming from ear to ear.

'Nice to meet you,' I smiled. 'How are you today?'

'Fine!' he boomed at us, then he said something else but I couldn't make it out. His speech was loud but the words were indistinct and I had to get my ear attuned to it. Finally I realised he was asking if he could see the horses.

'Of course,' I said. 'Come along.' I took him with me round the yard as I fed and watered, stroked and examined the horses, introducing him to each in turn. I could tell he had an affinity for them. He knew how to reach out gently without making them nervous, but he moved so slowly, shuffling his feet, that I wasn't sure it would be safe to leave him alone with some of the more restless ones. He wouldn't be able to get out of their way in time if they started acting up.

Edward was trying to say something to me and I was embarrassed that I kept having to ask him to repeat it as I strained to make out the words. I could tell he was getting frustrated with the effort by the time I understood that he was asking if he could work for us.

'Certainly,' I said. 'Do you want to start by sweeping the yard?' I handed him a brush and showed him the area I meant, then I wandered off to do some other chores, while keeping half an eye on what he was doing. I wasn't sure how capable he was of looking after himself or how much supervision he might need. He was sweeping meticulously, though, not moving on until each corner was spotless.

After about an hour I turned round and saw Edward sitting on the ground by his brush and I hurried over, alarmed. 'Are you OK?'

'I'm having a rest,' he said.

'That's fine. Let me know when you're ready for another job.'

'I'd like another job,' he said, standing up, and I realised that he had quite simply got fed up with sweeping – and who could blame him? I was busy grooming the horses so I took him with me and asked him to hold them steady while I worked. It was a useful way of observing his reactions around the animals, and I was impressed with his ability. He seemed pleased as punch to be working with the horses, and I realised that first morning that he was immensely strong – a quality that is always useful on a farm.

The highlight of the morning for Edward was definitely when the baker's van came round. He ran forward to get into the queue with the other staff members who were there that day.

'Do you have any money, Edward?' I asked.

'Of course I do,' he said, and he pulled out a £5 note with which he bought himself a cheese and onion sandwich, a pasty and a Coke, then he went to sit and eat with the rest of the team. I hung around and could hear them asking Edward questions and him replying. They seemed to be hitting it off.

'He's lovely,' they said to me later. 'What a great guy!'

I had a chat with Edward myself and he told me that he worked two days a week at a bookshop in town, where he served customers who were buying books or CDs, helped in the bookshop café by loading the dishwasher or cleaning tables, did some hoovering, and even went to the bank to get change. He was obviously quite capable of doing a range of jobs, and I also found that the more I talked to him, the easier it was to understand his speech. He was a friendly, natural man, very likeable and happy.

At one o'clock, a taxi came to pick him up and we waved goodbye but I had a feeling we hadn't seen the last of him, and I was right. That same afternoon there was a phone call from his key worker.

'Edward had a wonderful time and is asking when he can come again. Did you find him useful?'

'Very useful,' I said. 'We'd be happy to have him back.'

We agreed that he would come two days a week, on Tuesdays and Wednesdays, and that he would be dropped off at 8am and picked up again at 1pm.

'The only problem,' I said to Michael, 'is that I'm not sure what he's capable of. I don't want to humiliate him by giving him jobs he can't manage.'

'You said he's physically strong. Why don't we try him out with the Billy Goat?' This is a huge vacuum cleaner, which is used after mucking out to suck up the last bits of straw and droppings. I have trouble using it myself because it's so big and unwieldy, and it's tricky to start, like a hand-cranked lawnmower.

When Edward came back a couple of days later, beaming from ear to ear and obviously excited to be with us again, Michael went over to have a chat with him and explain how the Billy Goat worked.

'This could be one of your responsibilities every time you come,' Michael said, while demonstrating how to run the machine along the alleyways between the horses' stalls. 'Would that be all right with you?'

Edward nodded emphatically, eager to get his hands on the machine. We kept an eye on him that first morning, but he did an impeccable job, leaving not so much as a scrap of debris behind. He seemed very proud of the trust we were putting in him and later I overheard him boasting that he was 'in charge' of the Billy Goat. He was also delighted when we gave him his own Greatwood purple sweatshirt.

Edward was soon part of the Greatwood team, and we looked forward to the mornings when he was coming. We were happy to be part of the full life he led – working for us and the bookshop, often having supper with his parents in the evenings, but spending the rest of the time in the home he shared with three other lads. It was a good life in which he could be independent but supported, and his genuine love of horses meant that Greatwood was an ideal job for him.

It was a learning curve for us, though. Edward was our first volunteer with special needs and working with him helped us to formulate the strategies we would use with others that came in future. First and foremost, we would treat them as one of the team, giving them jobs and leaving them to carry these out to the best of their abilities rather than standing over them to supervise. We didn't have time for hand-holding. At the same time, we'd have to let them work at their own pace. Edward often stopped for rests, which was fine, and he wanted to come indoors as soon as it started to rain. He didn't like wet, cold weather. Who does? The rest of us had to work outdoors in all weathers because the animals needed us, but if Edward wanted to take a break, that was fine.

Sometimes he stopped in the middle of a job if he got fed up. Once I asked him to pull up some weeds that were poking through cracks in the yard, and he did a perfect job on about half of the area, then stopped.

'That looks great, Edward, but aren't you going to finish it?'

'No,' he said stubbornly, and no amount of persuasion would change his mind. Who could blame him? It was a boring job.

He made up his mind what he was going to do, and that was that. Once I asked him to paint some breeze-block walls and told him where to find the white paint and brushes. An hour later I came past and saw that he was painting the wall in our special Greatwood purple, which I saved for woodwork and signage.

'Oh, Edward! That wall's supposed to be white,' I told him.

'Gary told me to paint it purple,' he said, and carried on.

I went to see Gary, who'd been a long-time volunteer. 'Did you tell Edward to paint the wall purple?'

'No,' he said, puzzled. 'I haven't seen him all morning.'

I laughed. I think he just liked the colour purple and decided that's what he wanted to work with. It was more interesting than white.

At our next open day that summer I found out that Edward had a talent for painting. One of his hobbies was painting by numbers and he had completed some large, quite complex canvases by filling in the colours corresponding with the numbers in each space. He generously donated several paintings of horses to be sold at the open day and we raised £120 by selling them. He gave one to the novelist Jilly Cooper, who was there as a special guest, and she sent him a bottle of wine as a thank-you.

Edward loved the party atmosphere at the open day, rushing around proudly telling people that he worked at Greatwood and knew all the horses by name. The only slightly negative note in the day came with the raffle prize draw. Edward had bought a ticket and assumed that meant he would get a prize, so as the draw came to an end and he hadn't been called up to receive anything, his face fell.

'Where's my prize?' he kept asking, bewildered, as if we had cheated him, and I had to explain all about raffles and that buying a ticket didn't mean that you would win a prize. He was a bit puzzled but soon forgot about it.

Gradually I was giving him more responsibility with the easy-going horses, letting him lead them out to the field, or hold them steady while the farrier worked on them. He became particularly close to a horse called Tim, a pretty chestnut with a white blaze and an almost flaxen mane, who used to be a flat racer out in Hong Kong.

Tim was a perfect gentleman of a horse, known to all as Saint Timothy for his lovely manner. He had a couple of problems: first of all, he wasn't used to being turned out to graze, and there was a risk that, if left to himself, he could have gone berserk and rushed around crashing into fences, overwhelmed by the great outdoors. Secondly, he had bad feet and our farrier told us he would require specialised shoeing for the rest of his life. We found out that he had been involved in a multi-horse pile-up during one of his races and had clearly sustained some injuries. After careful thought, we decided that this ruled out rehoming him. He would stay with us for the rest of his life.

Edward was very good at holding and leading Tim, and also loved bringing in Tish when we had turned him out with Red. He loved this responsibility and got quite puffed up about showing off his skills in front of the others. There were some horses we couldn't leave him alone with, though, because he just wasn't quick enough to stay out of their way, and Red was one of them.

One day, I asked Edward to go and clear up some droppings that had been left in the drive, because we were expecting visitors. He completely misunderstood what I had asked and half an hour later, Maddy, who had become our absolute mainstay in the office, found him mucking out Red's stable.

'Edward, what are you doing in there?' she asked. 'I don't think you should be in there.'

'Helen told me to,' he said.

'I think you should come out now,' she said gently.

He then got cross with her. 'No! I'm doing my job.'

Maddy had to come and find me and explain the situation. I hurried straight up to the stable. 'That's terrific, Edward. Thanks for doing that. I've got another job I really need you to do straight away, though.'

Reluctantly he followed me back into the yard as I racked my brains, trying to think of another suitably urgent job I could give him.

Overall, though, within a few months Edward had become our favourite team member at Greatwood, universally adored. At our Christmas parties, he was the life and soul, joining in with the singing and dancing with the best of them. He's a very special human being, and is now officially our longest-serving team member. Over the last eight years, he has seen staff and horses come and go, and now no one has been here as long as him, apart from Michael and me.

The experience of learning how to work with Edward was important for us. It gave us more confidence that we could help people with special needs, and helped us to clarify the way we would work with them and the jobs we would be able to give them. Armed with these insights, we could go back to the education authorities and ask if they would like to send us any children with special needs to visit the horses. Greatwood was slowly getting ready for its next phase.

Chapter 8

Bobby and Bob

The first priority at Greatwood was to get the place tidy, settle in the horses, put the rehoming regime in place and do as much fundraising as we could. That huge debt incurred through the move from Devon meant we continued to walk a financial tightrope for several years, despite the generous support we were receiving from many quarters, and it slowed down our plans. Before we could start inviting groups of children to Greatwood, we also realised we needed more facilities – and an extra member of staff, because it was going to be too much for Michael and me to handle the administration, supervise the visits, and continue to run the farm and tend the animals as well. We advertised in 2005 and soon found a phenomenal woman called Elizabeth, who was in a position to take on some work now that her own children had grown up.

The first task we set her was researching alternative sources of funding, particularly from trusts, but right from the start, she and Michael spent many hours discussing the possibility of taking in pupils from local schools. She picked up Michael's enthusiasm and understood his vision about the way horses and children could help each other and his conviction that the horses had a remarkable reaction to fragile, needy children. From then on, the pair of them were on a mission.

Elizabeth was like a whirlwind blasting into Greatwood. She reorganised our computer files so that we could find documents easily without trawling through every last folder, she began to liaise with relevant authorities on our behalf, and she had a natural empathy with the horses as well. She was the perfect person to assist Michael in developing the scheme to work with children. Apart from anything else, she was already registered with a board called the Countryside Educational Visits Accreditation Scheme, and had been trained to conduct visits to farms for schoolchildren, so her experience would be invaluable.

'We'll need a classroom for a start,' she declared, and before long she had begun to raise funds to transform the old milking parlour into a meeting room and classroom in which the children could assemble to learn about the farm before their sessions with us started.

Michael and Elizabeth started to make enquiries at local schools and frequently disappeared off together to meet the teachers in person to discuss what Greatwood could offer to children with special needs. She had been particularly enthused by the story of Sophie and Darcy Day and was good at passing on her enthusiasm, so before long we had a list of schools queuing up to send pupils for a visit.

Together with Michael, she worked out a programme that visiting children could follow, starting with a general talk about how we operated at Greatwood, and warnings about safety issues round the farm, then leading up to the children being able to groom, muck out and feed the animals by themselves. Each session had a clear structure with a range of carefully planned activities that would allow the children to feel they'd achieved something by the end of their course. The programme was designed to teach them subtly about teamwork and respect for others, and to build up their confidence and self-esteem. Elizabeth understood that meeting new people and even the animals would be daunting for some children, and she painstakingly took photographs of every animal and every person to show to children at their school before they even set foot in Greatwood. We knew that the hands-on work was what seemed to get through to young people, but when dealing with children with special needs it was important to prepare them properly for it.

We'd been trying to come up with a name for the scheme but hadn't found anything that was quite right, when one day Elizabeth had a brainwave.

'Horse Power!' she exclaimed. 'That encapsulates everything we want to do in a nutshell.'

Michael was delighted – it was exactly the punchy kind of name we'd been looking for – and Horse Power it was from then on.

The first formal visit was scheduled for the summer of 2006, before we'd had time to complete work on the new classroom, so we erected a big marquee on the lawn in front of our cottage and carried out some tables and chairs to set up inside. I was apprehensive when I heard that our first visitors were to be half a dozen thirteen- and fourteen-year-olds from a residential school for children with serious emotional and behavioural difficulties. This bunch came from a place for disturbed children who had already been excluded from mainstream schools. It was going to be a leap in at the deep end, and we all mentally braced ourselves.

In advance, the school sent a short, written brief about the children, all of them boys. Some of them had attention deficit hyperactivity disorder, or ADHD, which meant they could be expected to get bored easily, to act impulsively and have trouble focusing on tasks. Elizabeth was warned that one child always freaked out if he was photographed, so she promised there would be no cameras around. Another one was prone to seizures, but the teachers accompanying them were trained in what to do if he had a fit.

It was daunting, but Elizabeth decided not to pay too much attention to the written report, instead taking the boys at face value once they arrived. When a new horse was coming to Greatwood, we often received an advance report about its past history and how it came to be in need of sanctuary, but we'd learned that no written document could give us any idea about what that horse was really like: how it moved, the way it communicated, its personality, its smell, its aura. These children might be in a secure unit because of their difficult behaviour, but they were all troubled individuals with unique personalities and we decided to try to view them that way, just as we would a traumatised horse.

We were expecting the children to arrive in a minibus, but a car came down the drive first, with just two occupants. They pulled up, the passenger door burst open and a small, wiry boy with long straggly hair jumped out, looked around, and shouted 'Fuck me!' at the top of his lungs.

His teacher hurried over to introduce herself to Elizabeth and explained: 'The minibus with the others is just behind us but Bobby here refused to get into it, so I brought him in my car.'

Bobby looked very pleased to have received this special treatment. He strutted round the yard, glancing into all the barns, and uttering expletives as he went, his sharp eyes checking out every nook and cranny. He looked like a scraggy little cockerel, trying to seem bigger than he was in order to hold his own in the pecking order.

'Oy, Miss,' he shouted. 'Why's that big horse in there with just the little one?'

He was staring into the barn that Red shared with Toffee. Elizabeth started to explain, but already Bobby's attention had wandered and he had moved on to the next outbuilding, and was peering in at the chicken coops. He was constantly on the move, not standing still for a minute.

'I hope someone gave him his Ritalin this morning,' the teacher murmured. 'He's impossible without it.'

At that moment, we spotted the school minibus coming up the drive and Bobby dashed over to open the gate, obviously wanting to demonstrate that he was already 'established' on the farm while they were newcomers. A stream of lanky, spotty youths sauntered off the bus, all of them going through that early teenage phase when they're trying to look hard and tough but in fact anyone can tell that if you scratched the surface you'd find a scared little boy underneath. They were much taller than Bobby, but that didn't stop him hurling expletive-laden banter – 'Oy, you got gel in your hair, ya fuckin' poofter?' – in his piping, not-yet-broken voice.

Elizabeth was beginning to feel as though we might have bitten off more than we could chew. These lads seemed uncontrollable, and she wasn't sure how she would keep them quiet long enough to tell them anything about the work we did at Greatwood. She was also concerned that if we couldn't control them, it might not be safe to take them to meet some of the more spirited horses.

She clapped her hands to get their attention. 'Everyone come and sit down for a moment while I tell you what we're going to do.'

They followed her into the classroom we had improvised inside the marquee and she handed out labels, asking them each to write their name on a label and stick it to their jumpers so we knew who they were. Her request was met by a long stream of Anglo-Saxon cursing, but most of them did as she asked. The teachers crouched down to help a few boys and she realised they must have problems writing. Elizabeth blinked; she hadn't expected any thirteen- or fourteen-year-old boys to be unable to write their own names. It was going to be a steep learning curve.

Elizabeth started to explain why racehorses need to do something else when, for whatever reason, their racing days are over, but she had already lost the attention of some of the boys, including Bobby. It wasn't a normal classroom, as demonstrated when a chicken strutted in to see what was going on, but these children weren't able to attend conventional schools and reacted against anything that resembled one. At that point, as if knowing that a distraction was called for, my little white Jack Russell, Mabel, burst into the marquee and made a beeline for Bobby. She jumped up and put her paws on his lap and he was delighted, stroking her and chatting to her in a sing-song voice of the kind people normally use for babies: 'Who's a lovely doggie, then? Aren't you a good girl?'

Elizabeth swiftly wrapped up her opening remarks and led the group out towards a large field where some of the horses were being kept. Getting all the boys to go in the same direction was like trying to round up a herd of excited puppies, but she managed, more or less. As soon as he saw us approaching, Steady Eddy trotted over to the fence where we were standing and Elizabeth began telling the boys his story.

He had originally been called Sunshine, but when he arrived at Greatwood Farm we already had another horse called Sunny and we didn't want to get them confused. For some reason, we started calling Sunshine 'Edward', which was shortened to Eddy, and because he was a steady horse, the name Steady Eddy stuck. We were told he had been a racehorse but unfortunately he didn't have a passport so we couldn't work out his full history. All horses are required to have passports to prove their identities. It helps to prevent horse theft, amongst other things. But Eddy had somehow slipped through the net and came to us with virtually no known history. He had a big, plain face, small eyes and small ears, and a lumbering, rather clumsy body, and he soon became one of the most popular horses in our yard, a real stalwart character.

When they saw quite how big these Thoroughbreds were, most of the boys huddled together a few feet behind the teachers, but Bobby was off in a world of his own. He was hopping, kicking at stones, jumping and spinning in the air, a never-ceasing tornado of pent-up energy. As soon as the group stopped walking, Bobby sat down on the ground and started digging into the soil and tossing handfuls of earth over his shoulder. Elizabeth decided to ignore him and address her remarks to the others, but she was soon interrupted by a teacher admonishing him.

'Bobby, stop eating the grass. It's bad for you.'

She turned round to see that he had some grass sticking out of his mouth and a guilty expression, and she was astonished. She could understand why young babies might eat grass if their mother plonked them down on the ground, but for a teenage boy to do it was extraordinary. Was it attention-seeking behaviour? Was he hungry?

She gathered her thoughts and carried on with the story. A few of the boys came forward to stroke Steady Eddy, and Tim, who had joined her, but the others seemed too nervous. They were joshing each other, stepping forward for a quick touch, then jumping back again.

'Gently does it,' she warned. 'Don't frighten them.'

A teacher pulled her to one side. 'I don't suppose there's anywhere they can smoke? They haven't had a ciggie for a while now and nicotine deprivation can make them more agitated than normal.'

Elizabeth was surprised yet again. 'But they're only children! Do they really smoke?'

'I'm afraid so,' the teacher sighed. 'Frankly, it's the least of our worries so we just let them. You have to choose your battles.'

Elizabeth looked around. 'We normally ask visitors not to smoke on the farm because of all the straw and other flammable material lying around. But maybe I can find somewhere …' She racked her brains and decided they could smoke by a bench down the driveway, far away from the animals and the straw in the yard.

When they were told they could have a fag break, the boys raced off at full pelt to fetch their cigarettes from the minibus. Bobby retrieved his from the teacher's car and Elizabeth watched as he expertly cupped his child-sized hands to stop his match blowing out in the breeze and sucked in deeply to light his ciggie. He held it between his thumb and first finger and sucked so hard that his little face hollowed with the effort of getting a nicotine hit. The other boys reclined on the bench to enjoy their smoke but Bobby danced around them, gesticulating with his cigarette, waving it like a baton and giving a running commentary laced with profanities.

Elizabeth took the opportunity to ask one of the teachers about his grass-eating. What was that about?

'He does it when he's feeling insecure,' she said. 'He's away from his familiar environment here, and somehow eating grass seems to give him some comfort. But obviously we have to discourage it.'

Her heart warmed towards this complex, nervous, highly strung little boy, who was sucking the last hit out of his cigarette as if his life depended on it, with wild eyes still roaming all over the place, on the lookout for hidden dangers.

After they finished smoking, Elizabeth gathered the boys again and started talking to them about the need for hygiene on the farm.

'Why do you think we wash out the animals' feed bowls regularly?' she asked.

There was a variety of responses – ''Cos dirt blows in' or ''Cos they dribble in them' – and Elizabeth explained that it was to prevent the growth of germs that can cause disease. 'That's why you have to wash your own dishes at home, so that you don't get ill,' she said, while wondering how many of these boys had ever washed a dish. Smashed them, yes …

'Why do you think we wash and groom the horses?' she asked next.

'To stop them getting whiffy …' one boy answered, holding his nose, and they all laughed.

'That's right,' Elizabeth said. 'It's not very nice for us when a horse is covered in stinky mud and it's not nice for them either. It doesn't feel very good. So would anyone like to come and help us clean the horses today?'

To a one, they looked terrified and tried to shrink away from her.

'We'll be there to help,' she reassured them. 'It's quite safe. I wouldn't let you do it if it wasn't.'

They were all quiet as they followed us down to the stables, clearly nervous about what was coming. She had their full attention as she demonstrated how to groom a horse, first using a curry comb to get out any caked mud, but not pulling so hard that it would hurt the animal. The boys watched carefully and when she asked for volunteers, a couple of brave souls stepped forward to take over the brushing. Once they saw it was all right and that their friends weren't coming to any harm, the other boys consented to pick up a brush and have a go at grooming. We made sure they stuck to the gentlest, most docile animals and worked in pairs, with one of the Greatwood team holding the horse and remaining right beside them at all times.

But then Elizabeth noticed that Bobby was hanging back by the barn door. 'Aren't you going to try grooming a horse?' she called.

'They're too big. They'd fucking eat me, Miss,' he shouted back.

She looked at him cowering outside the barn door and an idea came to her. She walked over. 'Bobby, I noticed earlier that Mabel the dog really liked you. I don't suppose you could help me by giving her a bath, could you? It's a tricky job because she hates being washed, but it has to be done and you'd be doing me a big favour.'

'OK,' Bobby said doubtfully, wrinkling his nose. 'What do I have to do?'

She got him set up with a hose, some doggie shampoo and a towel, and left him to manage the wriggling, squirming Mabel as best as he could. When she glanced over later, he was soaked from head to foot but doing his best, and Mabel looked a lot cleaner. It was the first time that day she'd seen Bobby focusing on anything and it seemed like a good omen.

'It's good to see him doing that,' a teacher told her quietly, 'because he has problems with washing himself. I heard that in one of his foster homes, they scrubbed him down with a kitchen scrubbing brush when he refused to have a bath. Unbelievable, isn't it?'

'Oh my goodness! Poor Bobby.'

He was rubbing Mabel with a towel and she was obviously enjoying it because she turned to lick his face, causing him to exclaim 'Yuck!' and wipe it off – but we could tell he was pleased.

When the visit was over, the boys had one last fag break then piled back into their minibus.

'How do you think that went?' I asked Elizabeth.

'Not bad for a start,' she said, 'but I'm exhausted.'

I could understand that. Looking after the boys was much more tiring than looking after animals. She'd already agreed with their head teacher that they could come back once a week for the next six weeks and, having met the boys, she decided to keep the classroom-based part of the programme as brief as possible, letting them focus on practical tasks. She hadn't had their full attention until she actually put brushes in their hands and told them to get on with it, so that was obviously the way to go.

All week Elizabeth was thinking about Bobby and wondering how she could help him to get the most he could from his time at Greatwood. He was scared of the towering Thoroughbreds, but how would he cope with a pony? We had taken on another Shetland pony at that time, a three-year-old by the name of Poncho, who didn't have a home to go to. We thought he might be a good companion for one of our horses, in the way that Tish and Toffee had been, but in fact he didn't settle into that role. However, at only two foot tall he was much less threatening than a full-sized Thoroughbred. He was a little black ball of fluff and quite a bolshy soul, like all our Shetlands, but Elizabeth thought it might be a good idea to pair Bobby with a rebellious animal that he could identify with, rather than a meek, timid one.

The following week, she took Bobby to meet Poncho, where he stood in the shade of some trees, and explained how to groom him. Bobby seemed wary at first, but he soon got the hang of it. She left him to it but hung around eavesdropping, and heard him talking as he worked. 'There you go, little man, that's a nice brush for you, isn't it? Does that feel good?' His calm, conversational tone and rhythmic grooming kept Poncho calm as well, and she was interested to note that not a single swear word passed Bobby's lips. His hands were gentle, but she noticed that his fingernails were bitten painfully right down to the quicks, a sure sign of anxiety. Life was one challenge after another for this young boy, and he felt he had to be constantly watchful for whatever bad treatment might be coming his way next.

One of his teachers came up beside her. 'That's truly amazing,' she whispered. 'He's been working on that pony for twenty minutes now, which I swear is longer than I've ever seen him apply himself to anything.'

When he finished, Poncho's mane was silky and tangle-free, and she could tell Bobby was proud of his handi-work. She complimented him effusively and he grinned. He knew he'd done well.

After the boys had groomed their designated animals, they were becoming restless so Elizabeth took them on a tour of the farm, and asked them to point out all the dangers they could see. They thought it was hilarious that we kept a rubber ring beside the slurry lagoon, to be used in the event that anyone fell in. There was much talk of 'shit' and 'crap' and mock-pushing each other towards the pit, but fortunately no one took a tumble.

They then reached the electric fence surrounding the horses, and Elizabeth explained what it was and cautioned the children not to touch it. This proved to be a tempta-tion too far for Bobby, who immediately stuck his hand out, then jumped back as he felt the light current buzzing up his arm. Perhaps it dawned on him then that instruc-tions were given in his best interests and were meant to be helpful, rather than designed to prevent him from doing something just out of spite, in case he enjoyed it. Perhaps not. I don't think any of them ever touched the fence again after that. The other boys laughed at him, though, and he didn't like that.

'This is fucking boring. When can I go and have a fag?' he asked, scowling and rubbing his hand.

'Not yet,' Elizabeth told him. 'Soon.'

At the edge of one field there was a small chestnut horse called Bob, who was wandering around on his own, looking disconsolate. She decided to tell the boys about him.

'Poor Bob has had a rough time of it,' she said. 'He used to win races, but now he's eighteen and too old to race. When Helen and Michael went to pick him up, he was tied up all alone in a scrapyard. He had a nasty cut on his front leg – that's the bandage you can see – and a back leg that looked all wonky, as though it had been broken and hadn't healed properly. He's been moved from place to place, because no one wanted him.'

A little voice chipped in 'Just like me', and she looked down to see that Bobby was listening intently to the story. 'We've got the same name.' He rolled up his trouser leg to reveal a plaster on his leg. 'And look, I've even got a cut on my leg as well.'

While she was trying to decide how to respond to that, Bobby shrugged and the defiant look returned. 'Anyway, when can I go and have a fucking fag?'

She quickly wound up the talk and announced that it was time for the fag break, then watched the lads gallop off to the minibus to retrieve their packs.

'What's Bobby's story?' she asked one of the teachers. 'Has he really been moved from place to place?'

'I'm afraid so,' a teacher replied. 'He was seriously abused in a foster home when he was very young – they're the ones I told you about, who scrubbed him with a scrubbing brush. Since then he's been in half a dozen different foster homes but none of them could deal with his behaviour, and that's why he's with us.'

'That's horrible. The poor boy.' Elizabeth watched him strutting in a circle around the other boys who were sitting smoking on the bench and realised that he didn't have any friends amongst them. He was cocky, bantering and defensive, never letting his guard down, and with the teachers he was spiky and difficult. If his life at the residential school was the same, then he must be a very lonely little boy.

Elizabeth decided to take Bobby under her wing and try to make sure he bonded with the animals as much as possible during his time with us, because he didn't seem to think much of human beings. In fact, she decided that on his third visit she would ask him to help me to dress Bob's leg, since they had so much in common. When the minibus turned up the following week, she watched them all traipsing off – but there was no sign of Bobby. Was he coming separately in a teacher's car?

'No, he's not allowed to come this week,' the carer told her. 'He's grounded.'

Elizabeth felt a huge sense of frustration, as well as anger, that our Horse Power programme should form part of some punishment. That's not what we were about.

Deterrents and endless recriminations don't work with horses and she was pretty sure they wouldn't work with a boy like Bobby either.

'What on earth did he do?'

'He escaped from the dorm, went out roaming round the grounds and set fire to a shed.' The teacher raised her eyebrows. 'So it's pretty bad.'

'Poor Bobby.' She imagined he must have been feeling very angry and upset. She thought about the comparison with Bob, our horse. If Bob had done something disruptive, such as bite or kick another horse, the last thing we'd do would be to punish a creature that had already been maltreated. It was totally counter-productive. She wanted to point all this out, but realised that it wasn't her place to interfere in their internal discipline systems. She was just upset that she couldn't do more to help that lost little boy.

The following week he was back again, his face pinched, white and anxious, and his ceaseless motion even more pronounced.

'Could you come and help to look after Bob?' Elizabeth asked.

'S'pose so,' he growled, chewing his fingers.

She gave him a brush and they both groomed Bob together, but she cautioned Bobby to be ultra-careful around the wound. 'One of the problems with horses – or any animals – is that they can't speak, so they can't tell you when they are worried or upset or frightened about anything.'

'Or sad,' Bobby chipped in.

'Well, remember that day when you first met Bob out in the field? We could sort of see that he was sad, couldn't we? But you're right – it's not always easy to tell.'

Bobby's brush strokes became even gentler.

'You're really good at that,' she said. 'Look how much he's enjoying it.'

For a brief moment, she thought she saw tears in Bobby's eyes. It occurred to her that seldom, if ever, was he praised for anything. He was used to criticism and punishment, not compliments. It wasn't the school's fault – they had to stop him harming others – but she could tell that this little boy would respond far better to positive reinforcement and personal attention.

From then on, Elizabeth made a point of telling the teachers, within Bobby's hearing, that he had a very good touch when grooming and that he seemed to know intuitively what the animals were feeling. She also tried to keep him busy, giving him one task straight after the other, and she never saw him eating grass again. The swearing continued to be as fruity as ever, but he seemed calmer and more thoughtful.

Elizabeth was sad when the six-week course came to an end and she realised she'd probably never see Bobby again. If only he could have carried on coming once a week ... but it wasn't fair to single out one child for special treatment, and the school couldn't spare a teacher to accompany him every time.

'You've been a great help,' she told him as they were being herded to the minibus on the last day. 'Thank you very much.'

He shrugged and turned away with a cocky gesture of dismissal. 'Whatever! Bye, Miss.'

Michael, Elizabeth and I talked a lot about Bobby afterwards. We were still clarifying for ourselves the way that the Horse Power programme would be run, but we agreed that we would always take each child at face value rather than judging them based on reports of what they had done in the past, no matter how shocking. We would focus on what each child could achieve rather than what he or she couldn't do, and try to point them towards activities where they would be likely to succeed, thus bolstering their confidence.

We also decided that it might be a good idea to introduce children to animals who had some kind of similar history to their own. It had been interesting to see the way Bobby responded to Bob, and it reminded us of how Lucy had become close to Freddy and Sophie to Darcy back down in Devon.

'I don't know if we need to match-make deliberately,' Michael said. 'I think they'll probably find each other.'

And he was right. That's the way it would prove to be from then on.

Chapter 9

Henry and Potentate

Elizabeth and Michael spent a lot of time trying to plan for all the different kinds of children that might arrive – but in fact, as they soon found out, they never knew from one visit to the next what problems might arise, and Elizabeth had to think on her feet and react appropriately as each new group came along. There was a basic course structure in place but she had to be ready to throw it out the window if it didn't work for any particular visitors.

I was being stretched in lots of different directions. I wanted to do anything I could to help to make the Horse Power pilot programme a success, but someone needed to supervise the care of the horses, so that remained my primary role. It was also important that I kept up the momentum on the fundraising front, making sure that our reputation was continually brought to the attention of the great and the good in the racing world, so that we were awarded the grants from the Industry that we needed to survive. I became friendly with a lot of the trainers and was pleased that there were several who turned to us first when their horses were due to retire. It was a huge compliment when a caring trainer decided that they trusted us to care for and rehome their prized animals, and I was always delighted to get a call from one of these guys.

A couple of years earlier, we had been approached by an elderly Somerset farmer called Jim Weeden. He'd owned several extraordinarily successful racehorses over the years but his increasing frailty was beginning to make him worry about what would happen to his horses when he died. He had never married and was a quiet, thoughtful sort of man whose life was completely wrapped up in his racehorses and racing. He asked us to take in and look after one of his favourites, Potentate, when he had to be retired, and we were delighted to help.

Michael and I grew very fond of Jim. He used to come and see us regularly at Greatwood and occasionally we went to Somerset to visit him. He always astounded us with his depth of knowledge of racing, like an encyclopaedia on legs. Jim asked us to promise him that when he died any remaining horses he had in training would come to us, so when the sad day came I wasn't surprised to receive a phone call from his executor saying that we were mentioned in Jim's will. He'd left a substantial legacy to be split between a charity called The Injured Jockeys and us, and we took on the care of his only remaining horse in training, by the name of Park Lane Princess. To the end, Jim's main concern had been for the welfare of horses and jockeys.

Potentate was a champion hurdler in his day, winning the Welsh Champion Hurdle at Chepstow in three consecutive years. When we picked him up, we found he didn't have any health problems – he'd never sustained any serious injuries during his career – but he was a serious horse, and a bit of a loner.

Which horse would we stable him with? It didn't seem to matter because Potentate wasn't bothered. We tried putting him in with Tish, with Freddy, and a couple of others, and he didn't bat an eyelid. He got on well enough with the rest of the herd but didn't make any particular best friend. Many of the others would throw a blue fit if they were separated from their 'buddy', but Potentate was quite happy on his own, grazing at the edge of a field, thinking his own thoughts.

The only sign of trouble came the first day it rained after Potentate's arrival, when he made his way to the shelter we'd erected at one end of the field. It was easily big enough for all the horses kept there, but Po began to whinny and push and shove at the others, trying to barge them out. He obviously thought that the shelter was there for him and him alone. Michael and I had to rush out to the field to separate the horses and prevent full-scale war breaking out.

It wasn't a one-off event though. Potentate hated the rain and he'd make for the field shelter as soon as the first spots started falling, but if any other horse tried to barge in, all kinds of grief would be let loose. We tried to solve the problem by building another shelter further along, but Potentate decided that both shelters were his and ran from one to the other, trying to barge the horses outside. In the end we just had to leave the herd to reach an uneasy truce. Some horses stood their ground against him, while others chose to get wet rather than confront him.

I found Potentate an easy horse to look after, letting me do whatever had to be done without a fuss, but it was hard to make a connection with him. He kept himself to himself and was quite happy so long as I did the same. Jim had specifically requested that Potentate should not be rehomed, so of course we honoured this request, but as a rule we preferred all our horses to have some sort of job rather than just be a glorified field ornament. Potentate was a steady, unexcitable horse, and I decided he could be part of our Horse Power programme. He'd be safe around children – just so long as they didn't try to get into his field shelter when it rained.

The next batch of boys that came to us from a special needs school were marginally better-behaved than the last. They weren't from the secure unit, and were children with behavioural and learning difficulties rather than particularly troubled individuals. They trooped off their minibus and over to the marquee, and since it was spitting with rain outside, Elizabeth decided to give them a little bit more of an introduction to what we did, complete with worksheets they could fill out. She could tell it was a mistake as soon as she handed them round from the look of terror on some of their faces. Despite being in their mid teens, it seemed many of them couldn't read or write.

'We're not going to fill these out,' Elizabeth back-tracked quickly. 'I thought you might like to have them in front of you to help follow what's going on, but if you'd rather just listen that's also fine.'

She talked through some of the problems our horses had faced in their lives, and the ways in which we tried to help them overcome psychological traumas. A couple of boys were whispering and sniggering to each other, and one was reading a comic under the table, but she decided not to intervene. It wasn't her place to discipline them unless they were actually putting themselves or others in danger. Then her attention was caught by a young-looking blond boy who was following every word with rapt attention. He had a soft smile and his chin was tipped slightly to one side, like those coy photos of the late Princess Diana.

Elizabeth was throwing out questions, trying to engage the boys, and the more confident ones were shouting out their answers, but not this one boy. She noticed his reticence and asked him a question directly: did he know what horses ate?

'Oats?' he replied tentatively, in a voice that you had to strain to hear.

'Absolutely,' she smiled. 'Mostly hay and grass but if they need anything extra they can eat oats, boiled barley and horse cubes.'

He gave a shy little smile.

'What's that boy's name?' she whispered to a teacher standing nearby.

'Henry,' she replied.

'He looks nice.'

The teacher shrugged slightly. 'It's hard to get to know him,' she said. 'He doesn't cause any trouble, though. Not usually.'

When they stood up to move out to the yard, Elizabeth was surprised to notice that Henry was a good head taller than the other boys – most of his height in his long, skinny legs.

'Is he older than the rest?' she asked.

'Yes, by a couple of years. He's fifteen, nearly sixteen, and they're all thirteen, but he's been kept back because of his difficulties with reading and writing.'

She bit her lip. It must be horribly humiliating for a teenage boy to find himself in a younger class. Surely that would knock your confidence? It would be difficult to make friends as well. As they walked across the yard to the stables, she noticed that he wasn't chatting or laughing with any of the other boys, but as soon as he saw Mabel the dog, he bent down to make a fuss of her and she yapped her delight.

Elizabeth kept an eye on Henry as they went through the morning's activities – meeting the horses, and learning how to clean and groom them – and kept thinking that she couldn't understand what he was doing in a so-called 'special' school. The other boys were acting up: jostling for attention, swearing, not paying attention to instructions, or throwing handfuls of hay at each other. Henry hung around at the back of the group, but he behaved impeccably and she knew he was listening intently to what was said because when it was his turn to come forward and identify the correct brush then apply it to a horse's mane, he did it perfectly, without hesitation.

Once he was working on his own, she wandered over to have a chat with him. 'You look as though you've been around animals before. I saw you with Mabel earlier, and I think you've made a hit there. Have you ever had a dog yourself?' As she said it, she wanted to kick herself. Obviously, he wouldn't be allowed to have a dog at the residential school he attended, and maybe it wasn't a good idea to remind him of his home life before that.

Henry just shrugged and said, 'No.'

She continued: 'You've got the knack with horses as well. You seem to know exactly the right way to touch them.'

There was a long pause. 'Thanks.'

She decided to test him: 'Have you met the goats yet?' They can be more pushy and obstreperous than the other animals and she wondered how he'd cope with being jostled and nudged by them, but when she took him over to their barn, he was fine. He didn't talk to them, as others might do. Instead, he reached out and scratched the tops of their heads, in just the way goats like. He was a natural, and she couldn't get over the suspicion that he'd been involved with animals at some stage in his life. If not, how was he so intuitive with them?

After they'd all finished grooming, they took the boys for a walk round the farm. They ran ahead on the way up to the fields, letting off steam, and Elizabeth grabbed the opportunity to question a teacher. 'What's Henry's family background like? It's just that he seems very well behaved, and I wondered why he's with you?'

She sighed. 'All we know is that there was a huge family rift and he ended up in care. He gets very upset if we talk about it.'

'Oh my goodness! I wonder what happened?'

'We'll probably never know the whole story.'

That was something I'd got used to with the horses. They arrived at Greatwood with conditioned responses and behaviours that they'd obviously developed in reaction to some past stress, but we never learned what had happened because they couldn't tell us. Why did Potentate shove all the other horses out of the field shelter when it rained? Why did some horses get so stressed that they started crib-biting, as Jelly used to do? Other signs of stress that I'd seen horses exhibiting included shuffling from one front foot to the other, waving their head from side to side (known as weaving), and continually walking from one end of a stall to another (which we call box-walking). Some horses try to bite and kick, preferring to go on the attack straight away, and I always wonder what horrible treatment has made them that way. A few horses will try to lunge at you over the stall door when you walk past, but I've found that if I don't react to this they stop eventually. But why did they start doing it? In most cases, we'll never know.

The horses came running over to greet the group as soon as they arrived at the fence surrounding their field, and Elizabeth told the story of how and why each horse had come to Greatwood. Although they had met some Thoroughbreds in the stable earlier, the boys were nervous of these huge creatures galloping across a field towards them, and they hung back at first until Elizabeth managed to coax the braver ones forward. They were eager for a stroke but scared of the big teeth they could glimpse, and she had to reassure them that none of these horses would bite.

'What races has he won?' they wanted to know about each horse. 'Is he a champion?'

They crowded in, dodging inquisitive noses, wanting to get close to the most successful winners, as if some of the magic would rub off.

Suddenly, the teacher to whom Elizabeth had been speaking earlier nudged her and indicated with a jerk of her head that she should look back up the path. There was Henry, standing at the fence, with his head resting against Potentate's nose. Both of them were completely still. Most people try to talk to horses and engage them on the verbal level that we humans understand as communication, but Henry just knew how to 'be' with an animal. We'd never seen Potentate stand still and close with a child like that. He was the loner of the pack, the one on the fringes. It seemed as though Henry had found his soulmate.

Elizabeth didn't interrupt them or comment on the scene in front of her, but it stayed in her head and she mentioned it to Michael and me later.

'It's happened again. Your theory about children and animals of similar natures finding each other seems to be working.'

'Of course,' Michael smiled. 'That old Greatwood magic is potent stuff.'

At his next visit, as soon as Henry got out of the mini-bus Mabel ran straight towards him, and he scooped her up for a hug. He sat quietly during the preliminary classroom chat but it was obvious that he couldn't wait to get out to the animals and, once they were in the yard, he kept glancing up towards the field where he'd met Potentate the previous week. Although the others were being set to work mucking out, I asked Elizabeth if it would be all right for me to take Henry up to the field to help me check on one of the horses, and she agreed. I wanted to see the interaction between him and Po with my own eyes.

On the way, I tried to make conversation but received monosyllabic answers.

'You seem to like horses. Have you ever ridden one?'

'No.'

'Have you been to a farm before?'

'No.'

'Did you enjoy your visit last week?'

'Yes, thank you.'

It was hard going. When we got to the field, I climbed the fence and went to have a look at Bob's bandaged leg. To my amazement, Potentate wandered straight over to see Henry. He didn't stop for long – just went over, had a sniff, let Henry stroke his nose for a while – then he wandered off again, but Henry seemed pleased when I rejoined him.

'I think Potentate likes you. He's not normally friendly like that.'

Henry just nodded, as if it confirmed something he had suspected, then we walked back to the yard and rejoined the others.

Elizabeth and I would have liked to have got to know Henry better during the six mornings he spent with us, but no matter how hard we tried, we never got more than polite monosyllabic replies from him. He wasn't a big talker. We could see his confidence growing weekly, though, as he was by far the best of that bunch at dealing with the animals. Mabel and the goats always made a beeline for him the minute he arrived, and when he groomed a horse it stood still and remained peaceful throughout. Henry was calm, so they were too.

He obviously looked forward to going up to the field to see Potentate. Usually they stood together for several minutes, but on one occasion, reminiscent of his behaviour on Henry's second visit, Po just came up, sniffed at Henry, then walked off again. Elizabeth glanced at him to see if his feelings were hurt, but he simply shrugged and remarked, 'He's not in the mood today.' He didn't seem remotely bothered, as if he understood because there were many days when he wasn't in the mood himself.

Despite his self-contained air, there was something very vulnerable about Henry that made Elizabeth feel protective towards him. Maybe it was the hunched, slumped shoulders, or the quiet wariness, or the fact that we never once saw him interacting with any of the other boys. She was astonished on the last visit when a teacher told her there had been some trouble at the school that week and that it involved Henry.

'He stole a big knife from the kitchen,' she explained. 'He'd had an argument with another boy that went too far, and seemingly Henry was planning to go and stab him. The boy came to us, and we managed to stop Henry and get the knife back but he was seething about something, and he won't tell us what it was.'

Elizabeth couldn't imagine him getting into an argument, never mind considering using a knife on a fellow pupil. It didn't fit at all with the big, quiet, polite lad she had seen on the farm. All she could think was that the provocation must have been extreme.

That day, Henry worked tirelessly, as ever, without drawing any attention to himself. He preferred animals to people, and we would never find out what had happened to make him that way. I don't think his teachers ever found out either.

'We'll miss you,' Elizabeth said before he left. 'The animals will miss you, especially Potentate. Do come back and visit us some time if you'd like to. We're always happy to have volunteers, especially ones who are good with animals.'

'Thank you,' he said with a quick smile, then off he went, at the back of the crowd as ever.

Afterwards, she wondered whether it had been a mistake to make that offer about coming back. She couldn't say that to all the children who visited us, because some couldn't travel anywhere without their teachers or care workers, but she knew that Henry was almost sixteen and he could leave school then if he chose. She worried what would become of a boy like him out in the world. Would he stay out of trouble? Find a career? Get a girl-friend? Where would he live? Despite everyone's best efforts, the odds can be stacked against children who come out of care.

Frankly, I never expected to see Henry again and put him to the back of my mind, but around a year later, I was in the stables one day when I heard a familiar voice behind me.

'Hello, Mrs Yeadon.'

I span round. 'Henry! My goodness! How are you?'

'I'm fine. You said I could come and visit one day, so I thought I'd drop by and tell you that I've been accepted to study animal husbandry at agricultural college.'

'Oh, that's wonderful news!' I wanted to give him a hug, but I knew it would only embarrass him. 'You'll be terrific.'

'Well, it was coming here that gave me the idea.'

'I'm so glad we could be of use,' I beamed.

He still wasn't able to make eye contact, looking shyly up at me through a fringe that was much longer now that he'd left school.

'Do you think I could go up to the field to see the horses?' he asked.

'Of course. Potentate's there.'

I walked up with him, and Po came over, probably to see whether we had any treats with us. Henry stretched out his hand and he sniffed it, gave him a cursory glance, then turned and walked off.

I looked round to see if Henry was upset about this, but instead he chuckled – a sound I don't think I'd heard him make before – and remarked, 'He's not in the mood today!'

'Come back and work for us after you graduate,' I suggested before he left. We haven't heard from him yet, but I hope that one day we might.

Chapter 10

Mark and Toyboy

'Where's the ketamine then?' snarled a chubby boy with dyed red, curly hair that was growing in black at the roots.

Ketamine is a powerful sedative often used on animals, but I'd heard it had been adopted in the clubbing scene by kids who enjoy its hallucinatory effects. This boy, aged just sixteen, was trying to show how cool he was, but he had a round, babyish face that was at odds with his street-wise persona.

'At the vet's,' Elizabeth told him briskly. She didn't want him to go poking round in the supply rooms thinking he'd find some there.

'Bor-ing,' he drawled. 'We gonna ride the horses then?'

'Are you an experienced rider?'

'Oh yeah,' he swaggered, and started thrusting his pelvis in a disgusting manner, which led his cohorts to fall about sniggering.

'Mark, stop that right now or you'll sit on the bus all morning,' a care worker yelled, hurrying over.

Elizabeth knew straight away what was going on. This boy was big, loud and rude on the outside, and the challenge was going to be to find the small, vulnerable boy on the inside. That would be the only way he'd benefit from his visits.

She had been warned that these children could barely read or write and would react badly to any kind of classroom set-up, so she decided there would just be a brief classroom session at the beginning and end of the morning, with plenty of time with the animals in between. It was important that they listened to the rules concerning safety when working with animals before they went to the stables but after that she took them straight out for a grooming session.

She watched Mark out of the corner of her eye and he started off well, but then something snapped. He dropped a brush, the horse moved and suddenly he shouted, 'This is pointless. Why the hell are we doing this? I've had enough.' He barged out of the stall, kicking his brush away, and stormed over to the door.

Elizabeth racked her brains, trying to think of a way to re-engage him. She wanted him to feel as though he was good at something, but what could she try? She remembered Michael's theory about matching animals and people, and tried to remember if there were any animals with the same kind of attitude as Mark. Then she had an idea. We had two new Shetland ponies, Toyboy and Aaron, and Toyboy was quite spirited, with a tendency to naughtiness.

'Mark, I wonder if you could give me a hand? I'm going out to catch the ponies and there's one, called Toyboy, who's always a bit tricky to handle. He doesn't like doing anything that doesn't suit him. You seem strong and capable, though. I bet you'd be a match for him.'

Had she laid it on too thick? Would he charge out into the paddock and be too rough with Toyboy in an attempt to prove a point? Seeing her heading off, one of the care workers tagged along as well.

'You have to win Toyboy's trust,' Elizabeth explained to Mark. 'It might take a bit of patience because he can be stroppy.'

'Patience is hardly Mark's middle name,' the carer remarked, speaking about him as if he weren't present.

Elizabeth wished she would go back and rejoin the others and leave them to it, but there was no polite way of saying so. Our policy was to insist that teachers or carers had to be present at all times.

When they got to the paddock she demonstrated how to put a head collar on a horse, then handed one to Mark and let him through the gate. Away from his friends, he wasn't brash and swaggering any more, but seemed determined to achieve the task she'd set him. He walked carefully towards Toyboy, keeping his movements smooth and non-threatening, but as soon as he got within touching distance, Toyboy darted out of the way.

'Try talking to him,' Elizabeth called. 'Keep your voice steady as you approach him.'

Mark did his best, moving slowly and calmly, saying, 'Here, boy, don't worry. I'm not going to hurt you.'

Toyboy sprinted across to the corner of the paddock where we were standing, which in our experience usually meant he was getting to the stage where he was ready to give up and let himself be caught. Mark crept up slowly, Toyboy lurched sideways, and the carer astounded Elizabeth by making a derogatory comment to Mark at just the wrong moment.

'That's one more thing you've failed at. You can't do anything right, can you?'

'Leave him alone!' Elizabeth cried, aghast. 'He was nearly there.'

Mark threw the head collar to the ground, opened the gate and stormed out of the field. 'It's effing boring,' he shouted over his shoulder, and Elizabeth just stared at the carer with her mouth open.

'That's him. Always a quitter,' the carer commented, before following him down the path towards the others.

It was the worst possible outcome. Instead of a tricky task that Mark should have been able to achieve, which would have boosted his confidence, he'd failed – and what's more, he'd been put down by someone who should have known better.

Elizabeth heard yelling from the yard and hurried down. When she got there, she found Mark involved in a punch-up with another boy, and two teachers trying to separate them. Fists were flying and Mark's face was red and twisted with fury, while the other lad looked scared and baffled. Mark had obviously needed to find some outlet for his frustrations and had taken them out on the first boy he came across.

Elizabeth was seething when she described to me what had happened.

'There are times when I get so frustrated. I would love to point out that it's not productive to talk to children in a certain way, but it's not our place.'

Mark was sullen and uncommunicative after that incident, and frankly Elizabeth didn't blame him. She was annoyed with herself as well. She'd have to try to think of some other way of getting through to Mark – a task at which he couldn't fail.

Before the boys left that morning, she gave them a challenge to think about.

'Just recently,' she said, 'we were offered five horses. We only had one place available at Greatwood, so Helen and Michael had to decide which one should have it. I'll tell you about the horses and I want you to tell me which one you would have chosen, and why.

'One of the horses was very old and had poor vision. It got scared of loud noises and liked to be kept indoors, in stables. One was a champion racehorse that had just been retired and was quite highly strung but very beautiful. One had been badly neglected and was very thin, with sores all over its body and a nasty infection in one of its legs. One was a family hack who had been well looked-after, but the family had fallen on hard times and couldn't afford to keep it any more. And the fifth was the youngest of all. It had been bred as a racer but never managed to cut it on the track so its owners didn't want it. Which one would you have chosen to save?'

They all started arguing. 'The sick one.' 'The champion, because then you can breed more champions.' 'The old one, because then you won't have to look after it for long.'

'Miss, what would happen to the ones you didn't choose?'

'They might have ended up at the knacker's yard,' she said, and there was a great intake of breath.

'I would have the family one.' 'I'd have the young one.'

'Do you know how much it costs to keep a horse?' she asked. '£100 a week. Do you get that in your pocket money?'

There was much nudging and laughing at this. 'As if!'

'It's not fair that only one of them was allowed to come here,' Mark suddenly shouted. 'That's a load of crap!'

'I know,' she said. 'But sometimes life isn't fair.'

'I think it's stupid!' he said, and stormed off towards the minibus, kicking over a broom that was resting against a wall. 'I'm out of here.'

The boys were still talking about it amongst themselves as the teachers shepherded the rest of them back to the minibus to head home.

While the others got on, Mark hung back and seemed anxious to have a word with Elizabeth. 'So who did you pick, Miss?'

'Who did you think we should have picked?'

'I think you should have taken the one who was sick, because he needed help the most. The others would all have more chance of getting another owner to take them on, but no one would want to have to pay all those vet's bills, would they?'

'Well done,' she said. 'That shows a lot of wisdom.' She was glad that something about the visit had engaged Mark at last.

At the next session, Elizabeth was careful to set him easy tasks at which he could do well. By that stage, she'd realised he had an overwhelming fear of failure. Goodness knows where it had come from, but if things looked dodgy, he would immediately go off on one, claiming that it was 'boring' or 'pointless' or simply that he'd ''ad enough'. He'd charge off, and one of the teachers would have to go after him because we couldn't have kids wandering around on their own unsupervised.

On his second visit, Elizabeth discovered another little habit Mark had developed – kleptomania.

'How many of these little hoof picks do you have?' he asked slyly.

'I don't know. Loads of them. Why? Do you need one?'

'No, I've got lots myself.' He pulled some out of his pocket. 'I brought my own with me.' He started giggling.

'Where did you get them?' She looked closely. 'These are ours, aren't they? Did you take them?'

He nodded, pleased with himself.

'Well, thanks for bringing them back. I won't tell your teacher if you promise not to pinch our things again.'

He couldn't resist it, though. Any small items left in his vicinity would disappear into his pockets, but I think we got most of them back because he couldn't resist telling someone about it.

'Here, you lost something, 'ave you?' he'd chuckle, holding up the offending article.

He didn't want the items. He wanted us to appreciate how skilful he was at purloining them without being noticed. And in fact, he was quite talented, once managing to take my reading glasses from my top pocket without me noticing.

'Could I have them back, please, Mark,' I asked wearily, when I noticed him wearing them himself. I had to warn the rest of the staff to keep their valuables under lock and key while Mark was there, and to keep a close eye on him. It was better to keep temptation out of the way than to give him any satisfaction, and kudos in the eyes of the other boys, who were obviously impressed by his bravado.

Elizabeth still wanted to get Mark back together with Toyboy. She had a feeling they would hit it off, but she knew he wouldn't want to be seen failing to catch him again. She asked Mark if he would come to the paddock with her to check up on Toyboy, and he trotted along quite happily beside her. Fortunately, they managed to slip under the radar without a carer joining them. When they reached the paddock one of our team, a girl called Susie, was already there, so Elizabeth introduced them.

'Susie has trouble getting a head collar on Toyboy as well,' she told Mark. 'Can you think of anything she could try?'

'I know,' he said. 'Why don't the two of us do it together, then we could corner him?'

'That's a good idea,' Elizabeth said, catching eyes with Susie. 'I've got a treat here as well. Why don't you offer that to him, Mark? It might help.'

With a combination of the tasty morsel, and the two of them closing in slowly and gently on him, Mark was able to get close enough to slip the head collar over Toyboy's head and he punched the air in triumph, shouting 'Yes!'

'Do you want to lead him down to the stables and groom him?' Elizabeth suggested. Once the head collar was on, she knew Toyboy would be perfectly manageable.

'Oh, all right then,' Mark consented, as if doing her a big favour.

From then on, Mark became very possessive of Toyboy. By his fourth visit, he'd won the pony's trust to the extent that he was able to catch him on his own, without any help. He told everyone that he was the only person allowed to groom Toyboy because no one else could manage him. This loud, stroppy boy spent long hours gently grooming the temperamental pony and there were far fewer tantrums after that. In fact, I overheard Mark telling one of his teachers that he liked coming to Greatwood because it was the only place where he felt calm. To me, that was a lovely compliment. It meant we were doing something right. I'd been worried that we would never manage to recreate the magic of the Greatwood Devon experience, especially after we lost Chic and Poppy, but it was becoming abundantly clear that the gentle, settled and happy atmosphere had come along with us.

Mark asked Elizabeth on several occasions about what actually happens at the knacker's yard. Did some horses have to go there even though they were still young, simply because they had problems and no one else wanted them? It was an issue that seemed to bother him greatly. For a child who considered himself ''ard', the empathy was astounding. Was he worried that he would end up in the 'knacker's yard' himself?

She answered his questions honestly and factually. A few thousand horses retire from racing each year and most of them are now retrained for another career, but if a vet feels that a horse doesn't have a reasonable quality of life, it is the kindest thing to put it to sleep. The 'knacker's yard' is just a saying. We don't actually eat horse meat in this country. At Greatwood we take horses that have got into trouble, and we make them better again and try to rehome them with a caring new family. Sometimes this is not possible, especially if they can't be ridden, but if they are healthy we give them a responsible job helping to look after children.

Mark's group finished their six-week course and as she waved goodbye to them, Elizabeth wondered what would become of him in particular. The noisiest and most demanding of the bunch, he was also the most needy. She had an image in her head of him balancing on a knife edge; with a lot of personal attention and guidance, he could have been guided towards an apprenticeship of some kind where he could have learned a skill that would enable him to earn an honest living.

It wasn't to be. We don't usually hear news of children who have been through the Greatwood programme, but in Mark's case, we did. Just two years after the time he spent with us, he was in a young offenders' unit. It seems he had been polishing up his thieving skills, the one thing he was proud to be good at. I still hope that somewhere in the system he will come across more adults who will see the vulnerable little boy beneath the hard outer shell, take him under their wing and build on the strengths that we could see. Fingers crossed.

Chapter 11

Zoe and Sunny

Just before we left Devon, Michael and I had managed to rehome two of our horses, Sunny and Steady Eddy, with a woman who had a smallholding in Cornwall. However, after we'd been in Wiltshire for a couple of years, we got a call from her saying that regrettably she could no longer look after them. Her health had deteriorated, and the horses, both in their early twenties, were getting creaky as well. Sunny had a touch of arthritis, while Eddy's teeth had all but worn away. She feared that neither of them would make it through the forthcoming winter in her wet and windy part of the world.

Both horses were too old to be rehomed as riding horses, especially as they were at the age when vet's bills were likely to mount each year. They were such good companions for each other that we couldn't contemplate separating them, and it would be too much to expect anyone to take on two veterans. Michael and I had no choice but to agree to have them back.

When they hobbled off the lorry into our yard, I saw a big change in them. Sunny had become a portly and very hairy horse, and both of them moved very slowly, stiff from the four-hour journey. We let them rest in a stable for the first day, but on the second we took them out to join the other horses in the field. Michael and I asked Susie to join us in case there was any trouble, as there can sometimes be when you introduce new horses to the herd. We needn't have worried, though, because an old friend of theirs from Devon – a horse called Monty – recognised them straight away. He came over to have a sniff, as if to say, 'Oh, hello, you're back again', then returned to his grazing.

At that point, the other horses in the field came galloping over to see who the newcomers were. This can be an intimidating experience and occasionally violence can ensue, but Monty lifted his head from his grazing and moved between Sunny and Eddy and the approaching herd. He showed his teeth, bucked and kicked, letting the others know that he was protecting Sunny and Eddy, and they all backed off. Monty led them up the field and became their protector from that moment onwards.

It was an odd combination. Horses usually pair off, as Sunny and Eddy had done, and won't let a third encroach on their partnership, but these three soon became inseparable. If we had to bring one of them in for a session with the farrier or to have a niggling injury treated, then we had to bring in all three or there would have been tantrums. Gradually, Sunny and Eddy started to socialise with the rest of the herd, but only under Monty's watchful eye. They were the old-timers – big, slow-moving, steady horses – and they had no patience with more spirited, foolish youngsters. Sunny in particular was a rock-solid horse and obvious material for interacting with children as part of the Horse Power pilot programme.

Under Michael and Elizabeth's careful stewardship, this was going from strength to strength. The new classroom was finished, so Elizabeth no longer had to teach in a marquee, and all the staff wore sweatshirts in Greatwood purple to help the children identify us when they came on visits. There was a set plan for each of the six sessions they would have with us, as well as Session Zero, when Elizabeth visited their school beforehand to explain to the children what to expect.

One particular school had children with complex social and communication difficulties, which made them very anxious about new experiences. The head teacher thought it would be beneficial for them to come and meet our animals, but warned that they would be extremely apprehensive about it. It was well outside their comfort zone. The week before the visit, Elizabeth went to their school with her photographs of the farm, several of the animals, and all the staff wearing their purple sweatshirts, and she explained who everyone was, and what would happen during the children's visit. They sat quietly and listened without responding a great deal, and she wondered how much they had understood. Would they be able to cope? We'd have to wait and see.

A minibus pulled into the yard the following week, the doors opened, and nothing happened. We were used to kids charging off, full of beans after the journey and curious to explore their new surroundings, but these ones didn't want to get off the minibus.

Elizabeth went to the door. 'We're just going into the classroom first,' she explained. 'You'll be able to look at the animals through the window but we'll stay indoors until you're ready to go out.'

'Will they bite us, Miss?' one little girl asked.

'None of our animals bite,' Elizabeth said firmly. 'And there will always be an adult right beside you at all times. Who wants to come and have a look?'

One by one they got up and let a teacher lead them the few yards to the classroom entrance – all except one girl, who huddled into the corner of her seat with her shoulders hunched up to her ears.

'Come on, Zoe. I'll be right beside you,' her teacher cajoled, squeezing her hand.

Elizabeth climbed into the minibus to see if she could help and she saw a skinny little eleven-year-old girl with her face hidden behind huge NHS spectacles, shaking with fear. She had enormous ear defenders on her head. The teachers had explained that some of the children with autism would be wearing these because they got easily confused by sounds they weren't used to, but they meant Elizabeth wouldn't be of much use because she couldn't be heard very clearly.

'Tell her we've got chocolate cake inside,' Elizabeth smiled, then backed off the minibus again to let the teacher try to coax her out.

Elizabeth started talking to the children inside the classroom, identifying any animals they could see through the window, and explaining that the barking they could hear was from a Jack Russell called Bessie, Mabel's mum, who normally sat in the office during the day licking any visitors, but who had been locked away on this occasion so as not to startle them.

After about ten minutes, she heard the door open and turned to see Zoe coming in, glued to her teacher's side. Zoe shrieked and looked as though she was about to turn and run when she heard Bessie barking, but Elizabeth quickly told her that the door was shut and she couldn't get out.

'Would you like to sit over here?' she asked, pointing to a chair.

Zoe tapped her teacher's arm. The teacher bent down and Zoe whispered something in her ear.

'She wants to know if she has missed the chocolate cake,' the teacher translated.

'We were waiting for you,' Elizabeth smiled at her. 'I'll go and get it now.'

This was the pattern. When you addressed Zoe, she whispered to her teacher, who then transmitted the reply. She couldn't look at anyone directly and shrank away when Elizabeth came near her. When I heard about this later, I sympathised because I'd been quite shy myself as a child, but this extreme level of shyness was an agonising affliction. It was horrible to see a child quite so handicapped by terror.

When the children had eaten their slice of cake, and the introductory talk was finished, Elizabeth opened the door and led them out to the yard. Fortunately the school had sent plenty of staff because some children, like Zoe, needed a teacher by their side at all times. The staff formed a loose circle around them and they walked along in the middle, shrinking back when some geese wandered past and panicking when Mabel bounced towards them. I quickly led her off and shut her indoors in the cottage because she'd have caused mass hysteria if she'd jumped up on anyone.

Elizabeth led the girls into the stables where some of the gentler horses were in their individual stalls, and she stepped forward to introduce them and ask who would like to stroke a horse. Zoe stayed right at the back of the group, clinging to her teacher's leg. Her eyes were big and round behind the thick lenses of her specs, and she was still wearing her ear defenders. If a horse made any movement at all, it sent her scuttling to shelter behind the teacher, even though she was several feet away and well out of range. All the others had plucked up the courage to give a horse a quick stroke before the end of that first visit, but not Zoe. She wouldn't come anywhere near.

'Don't worry about it,' one of the teachers told Elizabeth. 'When she arrived at our school, it was a month before she uttered a single word, and she whispers so quietly that it was about two months before any of us worked out what she was saying. I doubt she'll actually touch a horse while she's here. The fact that she got off the minibus this morning is a big achievement for her.'

Elizabeth wanted her to get more out of the Greatwood experience than that, but there was nothing she could do because no matter how friendly she tried to be, Zoe seemed utterly terrified and she always disappeared behind her teacher if she was addressed directly.

The following week, it seemed as though there had been some progress because Zoe got off the minibus with the others, and when they were all in the stable, she stood maybe a foot closer to the horses than before. Elizabeth got most of the other children to take up a brush and start grooming a horse. It's a very soothing activity and as soon as they started, and realised that the horse wasn't going to turn round and bite them or kick out with its legs, they relaxed and started to enjoy it. Zoe watched closely but wouldn't come any closer.

Elizabeth was standing outside a stall in which Sunny stood with his back to her, and watched the world go by. She ostentatiously stroked his glossy fur. 'He's the softest of all the horses,' she said in Zoe's direction. 'He's also the gentlest. He's like a big fluffy teddy bear.' She kept stroking. Zoe was watching closely and it was clear she was interested so Elizabeth kept talking. 'He's getting old and stiff and he can't run very well any more but there's nothing he likes more than a good old stroke on his back like this. He never moves a muscle when you're doing it because he enjoys it so much he doesn't want you to stop.'

The teacher whispered to Zoe, 'Why don't you go and give him a quick stroke?'

She thought about it, then gingerly stepped forward. Once she was within range, her little hand shot out and she touched Sunny's fur, then drew her hand back again. It was all as speedy as a frog's tongue flicking out, then zipping back, but for her it was a huge step forwards. Some of the horses don't like sudden movements like that, but good old Sunny didn't bat an eyelid.

Elizabeth carried on stroking and talking about Sunny and how much he liked to be touched, and Zoe came forward for another quick touch. Just two. That was enough progress for one day.

The following week, Zoe still stuck by her teacher's side, but she followed the group into the stable, stood closer than ever to the horses, and when Elizabeth reached Sunny's stall and asked if Zoe would like to stroke him, she came straight up and gave him a proper stroke right down his rump. It was time for the next stage. Elizabeth picked up a brush and showed her how to brush down in the direction of the hair, then handed the brush to her. She looked at it for a moment, panic flashing across her eyes, but then she reached up and began. Her first attempts were faltering, but when she saw that Sunny was still and calm no matter what she did, her courage grew.

Elizabeth stepped out of the stable, just leaving Zoe and her teacher in there. Zoe was gradually relaxing into the rhythm of the task. After a while Elizabeth went back and showed her how to untangle any knots in the tail, then once again left her to it. Never was a horse quite so thoroughly groomed by such a small person as Sunny was that day. From time to time, he shuffled a bit, but Zoe managed to step out of the way instead of panicking. She had finally accepted that she was safe, that no harm was going to come to her, and she let herself enjoy the task.

Zoe didn't even want to stop when it was break time and chocolate brownies were being served in the classroom, but Elizabeth persuaded her to come indoors. It was important that they all learned how to wash their hands properly after touching the animals and before eating food, and we also liked to use the break times to get the children into conversation and interacting with each other.

The group started discussing what they wanted to do when they grew up. One boy said he wanted to look after goats. Another said he wanted to look after sheep. A third boy, who had an American accent that he'd adopted from his favourite American TV shows, drawled that he wanted to look after horses. Someone else said she wanted to look after Mutant Ninja Turtles, but we let that pass.

So far, Zoe hadn't contributed during these sessions, but she seemed so much more relaxed than on the previous visit that Elizabeth addressed her directly with a question.

'Do you have any idea what you want to do when you leave school?' she asked.

She had to strain her ears to hear the whispered reply. 'I want to work with dogs.'

'I didn't know you like dogs!' Elizabeth exclaimed. 'You haven't even met our dogs. Would you like to meet them afterwards?'

'She's terrified of dogs,' her teacher whispered. 'She's more scared of them than she is of horses.'

Elizabeth decided to persevere. 'If you want to work with dogs, maybe you should meet Bessie. She's a lovely, gentle old lady. Would that be all right?'

Zoe gave an almost imperceptible nod and stood up to follow as Elizabeth went to open the door of the room where Bessie had been shut up for the duration of the visit. Zoe was breathing rapidly, obviously scared, but she seemed to be steeling herself to be brave. Elizabeth crouched down to pet Bessie and make sure she was calm. Zoe came forward and, finding her docile, she stretched out her hand and gave her a stroke.

'She'll love that,' Elizabeth said. 'Lucky Bessie.'

Each week, Zoe's confidence with the animals just kept growing. She was still scared of the dogs but she'd made a decision that she had to be brave around them and I began to let them out instead of keeping them locked away. She would shrink back a bit if they were barking near her, but she wouldn't panic. She began to answer questions in an audible voice and even to make eye contact with those of us she knew, although she would revert to shyness if a staff member she hadn't met came along.

Sunny remained her favourite horse, and she'd run straight over to give him a cuddle as soon as the group reached the stables, but she was able to stroke the others as well. Horses don't recognise shyness like Zoe's, because they don't judge people based on what they say. They form an impression based on the way people are with them, and they all reacted well to Zoe's gentle nature.

I watched Zoe skip round the yard on her final visit, and I marvelled at the transformation from the skinny little girl who'd been hiding on the minibus, too terrified to get off. She no longer wore her ear defenders and didn't seem bothered by the range of sounds, animal, human and machine, that filled the air.

'Hasn't she changed?' I commented to the teacher whom Zoe used to cling to. 'She's done really well.'

'It's made a huge difference to her confidence,' the teacher told me. 'Not just here, either. Back at school she has started putting up her hand to answer questions and volunteer information. That would have been unheard of a month ago.'

'I hope it lasts.'

We hadn't been going for long enough to judge whether you can make a real difference to a child's life based on six visits to the farm, but surely each new experience they mastered would help to build their confidence long-term?

Those of us who don't suffer from paralysing social anxiety will probably find it difficult to imagine the level of fear that Zoe had to overcome to achieve everything she did during her time with us. It was the equivalent of someone with vertigo doing a parachute jump! She went from sheer terror of the animals on the farm to being able to cuddle them – and, personally, I think that's pretty impressive.

Chapter 12

Different Ways of Communicating

The Horse Power pilot programme was being received with great acclaim by all who came on it. There were some children who got more out of it than others, but I think everyone enjoyed themselves at the very least. For most, it was the first time they'd had any contact with horses and they were amazed to find that, despite their lack of experience, the horses were prepared to take them as they found them. For children who had been stigmatised by being told they were too disturbed to be part of the normal educational system, this was very important.

So far, we had been visited by children who could speak and understand language. Elizabeth came to me one day and explained that we'd had an enquiry from a residential home for children with severe autism and related disorders that meant they couldn't communicate verbally. Was I happy for them to visit?

'What do they do then? How could they tell you if they need the loo, or if they're scared of something?'

'They each have pictures of little symbols that they carry with them, and they can take them out and point to them.' She explained to me that it was similar to a non-verbal language called Makaton, which uses picture-based signs to get meaning across. 'Besides, they would come with plenty of their own carers.'

I was doubtful. What would they get out of a visit? Would they understand when we explained to them why the horses were here, or how we looked after them? Would they be able to do anything, such as mucking out, or grooming or feeding the animals?

Elizabeth shook her head. 'No. Probably nothing like that. But the school feels they would benefit from being on the farm, walking around looking at the animals and maybe stroking them. Their teachers would work with me to see if we could develop any visual tasks for them to complete.'

'Well, if you're sure ...' I couldn't imagine how it would work because I'd had no experience of non-verbal children, apart from Sophie. But then I'd spent most of my life around non-verbal horses, so maybe that was a start.

The eight children who arrived on the designated day were obviously in need of constant care. There was a dark-haired boy called Mike, who whirled around in a state of perpetual motion, flicking his hand out at random, and when he got anxious he bit down hard on a plastic ring, similar to a baby's teething ring. There was Luke, who scarcely reacted at all to his surroundings but wandered around in a distant cloud of contentment, thinking thoughts that no one could fathom. There was Jimmy, who was obsessed with the colour blue. He found it a calming colour and wanted all the objects around him to be blue. He was wobbly on his feet so needed a carer by his side. Each had their own specific style of reacting to their surroundings, but none of them could talk.

It was a beautiful day so Elizabeth decided to start by taking them for a walk through the woods and the open spaces of the flower meadow, following paths that ran along the sides of the fields so they could see the horses from a distance. These children's responses to colour, sounds and smells can be heightened, and our meadows in summer are a sensory delight, full of buzzing insects, birdsong, glorious scents and brilliant colour. All was going well and they seemed to be enjoying themselves, when suddenly Mike took a wrong turning and started heading off down a different path from the rest of the group.

Elizabeth noticed what was happening first and went after him. She attracted his attention and pointed to the way the others were going, but Mike couldn't handle this. He had a meltdown, roaring and flailing his arms about wildly as he turned and dashed back towards the group. Unfortunately, one of his hands connected accidentally with Elizabeth's lip. The other children started to panic as Mike hurtled into their midst like an out-of-control automaton, and the staff from the home leapt forwards to encircle him and guide him away, back towards the farm buildings.

Elizabeth's tooth had gone into her lip and she was dabbing at it with her sleeve but she tried to adopt the calmest tone she could. 'All fine now. Let's go and see the horses, shall we?' She hoped that her voice would go some way to soothing them.

One of the children pulled out a picture of a sad face and showed it to Elizabeth, concern etched all over his face. She shook her head and smiled, even though it made her lip bleed more. She wanted them to know she was all right.

They finished their walk, and when they got back to the classroom, Mike was striding around looking at all the pictures on the walls. From a distance he looked older than his fifteen years. He was already sprouting fluff on his chin and could have been taken for a rather serious young man, but as you got closer you heard the strange phrase he kept repeating, that sounded like 'wiggle, wiggle', his own personal mantra, and saw the flicking right arm that he wasn't able to control. He didn't seem to have any awareness of other human beings or animals around him, except to panic if they encroached on his personal space. We could have been inanimate objects as far as he was concerned, and Elizabeth wondered how he would respond to the horses. Would he be aware of them?

She decided to introduce the children to Sunny first, because he was so steady and reliable. He wouldn't make any sudden moves that could alarm them. She asked us to clear the other stables nearby before she led the children out. First of all, Mike was led up close to have a look at Sunny and his flicking hand shot out but, to his carers' surprise, it was still for just a moment as it touched Sunny's coat. They exchanged a look of surprise, and one whispered, 'Did you see that?'

Mike moved on and it was Luke's turn to come and meet Sunny. When he saw him, this big old horse turned and lumbered towards him and Luke's face lit up as though he couldn't believe it. A horse was coming over to see him! It was an extraordinary reaction from a little boy who hardly ever showed any reaction to the world around him. Each of the children in turn came up to look at Sunny and all of them seemed transformed and animated by him.

This was quite enough for the first visit, but Elizabeth decided their response to the horses had been so positive that she could see no reason why they shouldn't try grooming the animals on their next visit, which was the usual procedure on the normal pilot programme. Their movements might be jerky and uncontrolled but she had a feeling they would all get something out of it.

The following week when the children arrived, she took them out to the stables to introduce them to the concept of grooming. She showed them how to use a mane comb to untangle a horse's mane, and a hoof pick to get little stones out of their hooves, as well as all the other brushes and how they worked. She then tested them, holding up each item and asking them to show which part of the horse it was for. Some could remember that the mane comb was for the mane, and that brushes were used to brush down the horses' coats. A few of them took a brush and had a go. Mike and Luke couldn't manage this but still they seemed to be watching. Mike wore his usual frowning expression and Luke gazed into space but there were no meltdowns and neither of them wandered off, and Elizabeth was beginning to learn that that was a result in itself.

Afterwards, back in the classroom, the staff got out the picture cards. They laid out cards with the symbols they used for happy, sad and angry, then gave the children some pictures of happy, sad and angry people, horses and dogs and asked them to match the pictures to the symbols. When it came to the people, Mike correctly identified the emotion they displayed and put them by the corresponding symbol, but when it came to the horses and dogs, he put them all on top of the 'angry' symbol. To him, something about their expressions or body language seemed angry. The staff were able to correct him by moving the pictures, including ones of Mabel and Sunny, to the 'happy' pile.

Next they talked about the foods that horses and humans eat, and this time the carers set up two symbols – 'like' and 'don't like'. They showed the children the foods that horses like and don't like, then handed them pictures of different human foods and asked what *they* liked and didn't like. When it came to Mike's turn, the staff were astonished when he put cheese, apples and sausages on his 'don't like' pile. They'd had no idea he had these strong dislikes. Sweet foods, such as cake and ice cream, went straight onto the 'like' pile – so no surprise there.

Despite his flicking, jerky movements, Mike was able to express himself quite clearly in this way. Our tendency as a society is to underestimate the capabilities of children such as Mike because of their obvious physical handicaps, but there was a brain working in there, and a personality shaping his actions.

On the third week of the course, Mike made quite a breakthrough for him when he managed to lay his hand flat against the coat of Tim, our elderly gent of a horse. There were no flicking movements, no 'wiggle, wiggle'; instead he just held his hand still and his expression was serene. Elizabeth was watching at the time, and she knew Mike was feeling the Greatwood effect. It lasted only a few moments, but it was powerful nonetheless. Even his habitual frown was smoothed away.

As a next step, one of the carers called Mabel over and tried to get Mike to stroke her. She stood amazingly still for a dog who might as well be called 'Off the table, Mabel', because that gets shouted at her more than anything else. She's a lively creature, to say the least, but she seemed to know that it was her duty to stand perfectly still as Mike and his carer crouched beside her. Would he be able to stroke her?

He reached out his hand but couldn't quite bring himself to touch Mabel. Instead, he caught hold of the carer's hand and guided it so that it stroked Mabel's head. It was a tentative, gentle gesture, and there was the ghost of a smile on Mike's face and a special brightness in his eyes.

Towards the end of the course, we invited the children's parents to come and witness what we had been doing at Greatwood, and we hired a photographer as well. Mike's mother had tears in her eyes when she saw him lay his hand on Sunny.

'I've never seen him so still and calm,' she said. 'That's beautiful.'

Luke's mother was also bowled over by his responsiveness around the horses. She said it was as if a light had been switched on inside him.

'I've finally found something we can do as a family. When he comes home at the weekend, we can all go to the local riding school. It's obvious he loves being around horses.'

To me, the boys' reactions had been very subtle but to their parents, they represented a huge breakthrough. We took photos of them all standing with Sunny and Tim and Mabel, and had prints made for everyone to remind them of their time with us.

Our first experience with non-verbal children had been an unqualified success and it showed us that we could be far more ambitious in the scope of the Horse Power programme. If we could invite groups of children with these types of special needs, as well as those who 'just' had learning and social development problems, we could appeal to a much wider range of schools and institutions. However, we would need some different types of programme so that whatever their level of ability, the children would be able to get something out of it.

Michael and I began to discuss the next stage, in which we would move Horse Power from its pilot stage into a fully recognised programme. He's always been the ideas person of the two of us. The whole concept was his 'baby' and, as usual, he was full of plans for moving it forwards.

'It's decision time,' he said. 'If we are to continue to invite children with severe problems, we will need to employ our own fully qualified special educational needs teacher. That's the only way we can make the programme work for children of all levels of ability.'

'I think we should,' I agreed. We were well established as a pioneering rescue centre for racehorses and it seemed this would be our next challenge. It was lovely the way the work with children complemented and enhanced the work with horses. To me, it was a perfect symbiosis.

Michael discussed his idea with Elizabeth and she agreed that it was a good plan to hire a special needs teacher. She didn't have the time or the qualifications necessary to take the programme forward to the next stage on her own, but she was as keen as us for it to develop and expand so we could offer places to as many different children as possible.

We placed an advert for a teacher in the county's education publication and were astonished at the number of applicants. So far, Greatwood was unknown in the educational field but the job description was unique. How many people could fulfil all the qualifications needed and be good with animals as well? We interviewed a few candidates and selected one, who came to us for a few months but then moved on, so we re-advertised, and once again received loads of applications.

Michael and I interviewed the shortlisted candidates ourselves and were particularly impressed with a woman called Hilary. She'd taught at a mainstream school in east London, then retrained as a special needs teacher, specialising in working with children who had behavioural difficulties. Her last post had been in a school for children with quite complex learning difficulties, ranging from severe dyslexia to autism to foetal alcohol syndrome and ADHD. She was a horse-lover who had been riding and looking after Thoroughbreds since childhood, and she had a degree in zoology. That ticked all the boxes, as far as we were concerned. It was impossible to think of a more suitable candidate for the post.

Hilary was a slight woman with curly brown hair and intelligent eyes that took everything in at first glance. When she drove to Greatwood to meet us, she wasn't fazed by the geese that rushed into the path of her car as she pulled into the yard, or Mabel jumping up onto her knee, or the horse hair all over the chairs. She was quietly spoken, but clearly confident in her ability.

She told us that she first began to have an idea that animals could benefit children around thirty years ago when she watched an American documentary about Mustangs being given to troubled children. The children were told they had to look after these horses, who are not the most compliant of animals, and that they couldn't give up no matter what or the horses would suffer. It taught them a real sense of personal responsibility that had a positive impact on the rest of their lives.

Hilary told us that in her experience, conventional academic schooling had a negative effect on some children, leaving them constrained and repressed, but when they were given a chance to do more practical tasks, they could shine.

'It's always been an interest of mine, and that's why I applied as soon as I saw the ad for the job here.'

'How much do you like to find out about the children you'll be teaching before meeting them?' Michael asked.

'The children that come to us will be referred by either teachers or parents,' she replied. 'I will have to know and understand any issues that they have beforehand, but as time goes on I will make my own assessment. I need to know in advance if there are any health issues, such as an allergy to wasp stings, or a heart murmur, or epilepsy, but if they're terrible at spelling, I'll find that out later.'

That's exactly the way we approached things. We took everyone at face value, rather than reading long reports about what they had done in the past.

'How would you manage badly behaved, unruly children?' I asked.

'If you keep children busy, they're less likely to misbehave,' she answered. 'I don't actually tell children off, but I'll try to point out a different way of behaving and let them know that they could make that choice.'

I smiled. I bet she was very effective. She was clearly extremely capable in her field and we knew from her CV that she was well respected within her peer group.

Michael obviously agreed with me because he said, 'I suppose our only other question is, when can you start?'

We could sense her enthusiasm for what we were doing at Greatwood. She could see how much difference the Horse Power programme might make to children's lives, and she was willing to come on board and help us to develop it. We were over the moon when she agreed to start at the beginning of the next school year.

We used the summer holidays to get the classroom all ship-shape for her. The old milking parlour floor was made good and carpeted, the office area was extended and we put in another loo. Some of the children who'd visited already hadn't been very patient at waiting to take turns for our one and only loo, so that seemed essential. We also needed an extra wash basin so they could clean themselves up after handling the animals.

We'd agreed that Hilary could have a free hand in developing the Horse Power programme in a way that would fit in with the Greatwood ethos. Elizabeth would continue to take a proactive role during a handover period, when she would explain about the work we'd done so far with children, and also about the rescue work with the horses. Michael and I watched them sitting chatting, with their heads together, and knew we'd made the right decision.

Chapter 13

The Baptism of Fire

In the months before Hilary's arrival, we had some new additions to our team at Greatwood. The first of these was a trainer called Robbie, an accomplished horseman who had worked all his life in racing. We had met him a couple of years earlier when he asked us to take in his ex-racehorse, Sunshine Boy. Sunshine had been a particular favourite of his, and a successful horse on the track with a number of wins notched up, but he'd succumbed to tendon problems and they'd had no choice but to retire him at the age of nine.

We managed to rehome Sunshine briefly but he didn't settle, so he came back to us and we tried to work out the best thing to do for him. He's a lovely horse, very nosy, and whenever anyone goes past he sticks his head up like a periscope to get a proper look at them. His other idiosyncrasy is a love of the most unlikely things, such as cups of coffee, bags of sweets, and even cheese and onion pasties. Woe betide anyone who forgets this, as your lunch will disappear if left anywhere within his reach. Robbie got into the habit of dropping by whenever he was passing, bringing a stock of goodies in his pocket to offer to his old friend.

Slowly but surely we managed to lure Robbie into the Greatwood net. One day he idly mentioned that he'd be happy to clear out the gutters for us while he was there. They hadn't been touched in years and some were so clogged up that tall weeds sprang decoratively out of them. Over the next few weeks, Robbie became a familiar sight round the yard, scrambling onto high roofs and leaning down precariously to scoop out ancient filth. Understandably, he was given the nickname 'Gutterman'.

Over the winter, when he knew that we needed extra pairs of hands, Robbie often came round at weekends to help us keep on top of all the chores. He was kind and gentle with the horses, had a particular knowledge and talent for backing youngsters, and, on top of all of that, was funny, generous and good-natured. Michael and I knew we wanted Robbie on the team but he already had a job, so it took us six months of cajoling, bribery and ultimately blackmail to persuade him to jump ship and come to work for us part-time.

Robbie's presence made a huge difference from the word go. He was popular with all the other staff, interested in the Horse Power programme and happy to help out when we had groups of visiting children – and the horses loved him as well. He soon bonded with Edward, and banter used to fly backwards and forwards between the pair of them, although once it went a little too far for Edward's liking.

Edward could take offence if he felt people were laughing at him – which was fair enough, if it were true. One day we got a phone call from his key worker, saying that Edward didn't want to come that week.

'What's the matter?' I asked. I knew he suffered from frequent bouts of ill health and hoped it wasn't anything serious.

'He says someone called Robbie was laughing at him.'

'Oh dear, I'm sure he didn't mean to,' I said. 'I'll check with him and call you back.'

Robbie was amazed when I mentioned the phone call but he knew straight away what was being referred to. 'Do you remember a couple of weeks ago when Edward had a headache and a bad tummy, and he told us it was a hangover?'

'Yes …' He'd mentioned it almost as though it were a badge of honour, as if he were one of the gang.

'Well, last time I saw him he looked a bit peaky and I said, "You haven't been drinking too much again, have you?" He laughed at the time, but later on I got the impression he was avoiding me. I bet that's why he thinks I was laughing at him.'

I called the key worker back and she confirmed that's why Edward was upset. He thought Robbie was teasing him about drinking too much. After a bit of persuasion, he agreed to come to work as usual, so long as Robbie would say sorry, which we arranged, and the pair were soon best of friends again.

The number of horses coming to us was increasing, and the workload just got greater all the time. Despite Robbie taking over on a part-time basis as our chief trainer, the main responsibility for horse welfare still fell squarely upon my shoulders. I didn't really have anyone else who was instinctive or knowledgeable enough to deal with the wide variety of health issues that arose. As well as looking after our rehomed horses on the farm, I was constantly giving advice on the telephone to people who had problems with their horses.

I had to try to juggle equine first aid with going to meetings and fundraising. I was increasingly being asked to make speeches at fundraising events, talking about the work we were doing at Greatwood, and that was a learning curve in itself. I didn't mind chatting in front of a television camera, but standing at a microphone with two or three hundred people gazing at me expectantly could leave me with a racing heart and sweaty palms. Sometimes it went well, sometimes not so well, and I never quite knew which way it would go before I stood up, but it was important that there was someone presenting our case to the racing world and beyond.

I could tell the efforts were paying off when we organised a fundraising dinner at London's Hurlingham Club in 2005. There was an auction led by Clare Balding and the guest list was basically a *Who's Who* of racing. I looked round the room and felt very proud of how far Michael and I had come from our humble beginnings in Devon just a decade earlier – but the achievement came at a cost. If I ever managed to earmark a clear day when I thought perhaps I could relax or go out to visit friends and family, invariably I would be called in at the last minute to resolve some problem or other in the yard.

Of course, over the years, this had become totally normal and I didn't in any way resent it. It was just that the charity was rapidly expanding and I was becoming aware that in order to continue to succeed, I had to share my workload. Our long-serving volunteer Gary had joined us full-time, but I think the responsibility and strain of leading an equine team were beginning to tell even upon him. He was a wonderful friend and steady ally but I knew that we needed to find someone else to take the helm. So when a pretty, slender girl called Sue came round asking if we had any vacancies, I gave it serious consideration. I could tell immediately that she was instinctively kind and gentle. She had looked after racehorses in training for friends of ours, so I already knew that she was loyal and trustworthy. The only thing that slightly concerned me was whether she would be strong enough to lead a team. Was she prepared to make difficult decisions or was she too nice for that?

'Why do you want to leave racing?' I asked. 'I'm worried that you'll find this work different in many aspects. For example, despite our best efforts we do have to say goodbye to horses if there is nothing further that can be done for them.'

Sue said that she understood that this was an essential part of horse welfare and although she, like everyone else, would find it difficult and probably heartbreaking, she knew it would have to be a necessary and vital part of her work.

She had spent most of her life working in racing but had become disenchanted with certain aspects of the Industry. As time went on, she couldn't bear it when a horse she had worked with was injured or even killed on the racecourse, and she tended to get close to the horses and missed them badly when they were sold.

I worried that she would find our work slower and less exciting than working with racehorses at the peak of their careers, but I decided to take the risk and offer her the job. And we never looked back, because she took to Greatwood like the proverbial duck to water.

The day-to-day management of the horses was pretty similar to what happened in a racing yard. They all had to be mucked out, exercised and groomed, as well as prepared for weekly visits from the farrier and vet.

However, we didn't have the time pressures of keeping each horse racing fit. Although we had to get the horses fit in preparation for a new home and a new career, if the weather was particularly ghastly, with horizontal rain and gale-force winds, we could have the luxury of leaving them in their warm and dry stables. But similar to a racing stable, we did have some pressures because the more work we put into the horses, the more successful our efforts to rehome them were likely to be. We would then be able to take in and help more horses – which could be a long process.

Racehorses are kept in a particular way, with a strict diet and training routine, and generally they have forgotten about being put out in a field or mixing with a herd, so retirement can be a big change for them in all sorts of ways. The first thing I want to do when a horse comes to Greatwood is to let it be a horse again. They need to feel secure in their surroundings, so I give them time in a stable to calm down, have all the necessary veterinary checks, and start changing their diet to predominantly grass and hay, which they may not have had before. If a horse is malnourished when it reaches us, we feed it appropriately and carefully to build it up. Any injuries are treated and they undergo a worming programme. They will also be assessed to see whether there are joint problems that could prevent them being ridden again, or if there is anything wrong with their heart, lungs or eyes. In these cases, we won't be able to retrain the horse for a new owner and it will have to spend its retirement years in our sanctuary.

When I first put a new horse out into a field, I sometimes give it some sedative first of all because otherwise they can get over-excited and start belting around, running at fences. More often than not, our existing herd offers a collective whinny of welcome, and the new horse will whinny back and feel a bit more secure. Chic and Poppy had been instrumental in helping to create a welcoming atmosphere in Devon, but it's still around in Wiltshire without them.

After that, I'll just leave the horse to settle in until I feel that it's ready for retraining. There's something I call the 'black eye', when a horse has withdrawn into itself, and it is only when I can see a glimmer and shine in their eye again that I think I can bring them in to work. At that point we'll start very gradually, with maybe just five minutes a day at first, and we'll go right back to the beginning, which means lunging and long reining the horse without anyone on its back, just teaching it the basics, such as going forwards. We do this in an enclosed ring so that it can't run off.

Only when the horse is comfortable with this stage will Robbie attempt to ride it for the first time and see how it copes. I used to have to do this stage myself but was quite happy to hand it over to him. It can be a time-consuming process in some instances, and time is what I don't generally have.

Once the horse is happy to be ridden in our school, it will be taken out into the yard to get used to all the other animals there, and then they'll go out for a hack on some main roads to become accustomed to cars, tractors and lorries. We need to prepare the horses for anything they might face in the outside world before attempting to rehome them. All the time we will gradually build up the length of the training session so they get used to working and know what is expected of them, but the main thing for me is that the horses are happy. That's always been the number one priority.

Sue was quick and clever, and within no time she had taken on board the Greatwood ethos and the way we worked with our animals. In her new role as equine welfare manager, she had to work alongside me and learn the way I liked to operate. I taught her my personal methods of running the yard – how to dress wounds, how to administer drugs, how to give injections, how to understand and pick up the moods of happy or unhappy horses, and how to put rescued and neglected horses back on the road to recovery – and after that I knew I could go away and leave her to look after the farm without losing any sleep. I was confident she would ably manage any crisis that should befall us, whether it was a burst water pipe, a poorly horse or a delivery of vital supplies that didn't turn up. Within weeks of her arrival, I trusted her to manage virtually every aspect of the farm, freeing me up to focus on other tasks, such as some much-needed fundraising.

A couple of weeks after Sue joined us, I decided to do home checks on some of the horses we had rehomed. It's something we have to make time for, to make sure that both carers and horses are well and happy. I set off, with Michael as my driver, armed with bundles of maps to help us to find the remote farms and stables where our horses had ended up.

We had already visited a couple of horses, who had been gratifyingly pleased to see us, and one of our last stops of the day was at the new home of a horse called Lola. Her carer was going to be out at work but we'd arranged that I would let myself into the yard. It was dark and raining by the time we got there and I was pleased to note that she was already tucked up in her stable. I couldn't see very well in there so I fetched a torch from the car and when I got back I noticed that Lola hadn't moved at all. I walked round for a better look and realised that her legs were unbearably hot and swollen. She couldn't bear me to touch them. She was breathing heavily and had a raised temperature, which could have been because of an infection, or the pain, or both. I always carry painkillers and dressings with me, so I treated her and made her a little more comfortable, but we couldn't arrange transport until the following day, so I had no option but to leave her.

The carer was upset when I spoke to her. It transpired that she had been turning Lola out into a field that had been grazed by cows and the over-use had resulted in deep areas of mud into which she had been sinking. The carer had tried to shield her legs with udder salve, but this just sealed in the infection. She hadn't wanted to call me for advice in case I took Lola back. I almost always try to solve any problems so the horse can stay in their new home, but in this case I had no choice but to remove her. She was simply too ill.

It was a racing day the next day and our usual horse transporters didn't have any spare lorries so we would have to use a trailer. I'm not a great fan of trailers, since one tipped over with two horses inside while I was driving. They weren't hurt but it made me paranoid and I've never towed a trailer since. My brother Matt was staying with us at the time and he agreed to tow Lola home for me. I asked Sue and Gary to come along too, in case we needed help with the loading and unloading, little realising that the day would be a baptism of fire for Sue, who was still only two weeks into her new job.

When we arrived, Lola seemed a little more comfortable and was easy to load into the trailer, but as we drove off, she began stamping around. We were on a bumpy track ridden with potholes and Matt was doing his best to avoid them. We hoped she would settle down when we reached the main road but instead she got worse. As we drove through the town of Devizes, Lola was crashing about so much that the trailer was rocking from side to side and passersby were stopping to stare. The noise she was making must have made them think we were towing a rampant rhinoceros.

I realised we weren't going to make it back to Great-wood, so I instructed Matt to turn into the car park of a nearby vets' practice I knew, where they used to look after our small animals for us. I dreaded opening the door of the trailer. Poor Lola was soaked in sweat, her eyes were wide and frightened and, worst of all, the inside of the trailer was covered in blood. We unloaded her and she stood trembling in the car park while startled elderly ladies came and went carrying small dogs and cats in cages.

The vets telephoned an equine vet to come over and brought out some duvets with which to cover Lola while we waited. On arrival, the vet gave her a mighty dose of sedative and painkillers, and then he called in some favours to arrange a lorry to take us the rest of the way. Gary and I travelled with her, and those five miles were probably the longest of my life as we had to keep holding Lola up to stop her falling. Every bend in the road presented a new challenge for our combined strength and sense of balance.

When we finally got home and examined Lola, we worked out where the blood had come from. Despite wearing travelling boots, she had managed to stand on the side of one hoof, severing half of it. We cleaned and dressed the wound and then, to make her as comfortable as possible, we brushed her to remove the dried sweat. Finally, we put on her rug. Far from seeming traumatised by the day, Lola turned round and gave a loud shout, as if to say, 'Well, thank goodness that's all over, but where the devil is my dinner?'

Sue looked very shaken, though. Imagine having to go through a day like that when you're only two weeks into a new job! I soothed her by telling her that this was a once-in-a-blue-moon occurrence and that it was highly unusual for us to use trailers. Racehorses are used to lorries and many of them have never been transported in a trailer. In normal circumstances we would never risk it.

Lola was put on strong medication to clear up the infection in her legs and her hoof healed slowly. Once she was completely recovered, we brought her in to work with Robbie and began to try to find her another home. I had ridden her before she had been rehomed the first time so I knew her to be a good, reliable horse.

Shortly after that, we were asked to appear in a television news item, which I was delighted to do, as it would help to generate some good publicity and possibly spur some extra donations. When the television crew arrived, I asked Robbie to ride Lola into the school to do a little flat work then take her over a couple of jumps. It should have been straightforward for someone of Robbie's experience but I hadn't taken account of the fact that a new pen had been erected at the end of the school, and for some reason Lola took violent objection to it. She objected even more strongly to the fluffy microphone at the end of the sound man's pole, and as Robbie led her to the round pen, she shot off in one direction while he went flying in the other.

'Oh no!' exclaimed the television interviewer. 'I can assure you that this won't be aired.'

But it was, much to Robbie's dismay, and he still gets teased about it to this day. Like Sue, he'd had a baptism of fire in the new job but it obviously didn't affect him too badly. He even agreed to work full-time soon afterwards. I'm glad to say they are both still valuable members of the Greatwood team to this day.

Chapter 14

A Fear of Men

All the Greatwood staff had to chip in and help when we had groups of visiting children. I often asked them to hold a horse steady so that a child could groom it, or perhaps have a chat with the children about their role in the charity. At first we worried that these professional horse people might feel it was more than they'd signed up for to help with visiting children, but they rose to the challenge without so much as a murmur, and their interaction with the children could be invaluable. I wanted every team member to feel involved with the charity as a whole and sometimes, if it was appropriate, we would let them know if there had been a particular breakthrough with a child; for example, 'Alistair just laughed for the first time since his mum died' or 'Helena managed to answer a question in class today.' I wanted us all to feel proud of what we were achieving.

There were inevitably some awkward moments when there was a clash between the running of the farm and the children's tours round the fields and stables, but we just had to manage these as best we could. For example, after mucking out we used a quad bike to push everything along the concrete paths to the slurry lagoon. It was quicker than loading it all into wheelbarrows – and not nearly as backbreaking for the staff – but it meant that the path was out of bounds during the process, until it had been cleared and cleaned again, and the children could find themselves stuck in the classroom for an extra half an hour. We tried to avoid it happening but by this stage we had fifty horses to manage and life can get complicated when you put them in the same space as unpredictable groups of children.

Elizabeth stayed to work alongside Hilary for a hand-over period and after she left, she remained a good friend of ours, often getting in touch. Hilary had to be allowed to make the job her own, though, and one of the first things she did was to decorate the newly lined classroom walls with pictures and short biographies of the horses, colourful charts about the routine on the farm, and some horsey accessories, such as old saddles and head collars. It became a professional-looking classroom, with plenty to look at, instead of just being a holding space where we did our introductory and closing talks.

Hilary was able to get in touch with councils and special schools within quite a wide radius and talk to them about her own experience, as well as the Horse Power programme. She asked that there should be no more than eight children in any one group, but said that where there were particular issues to address, she'd be happy to have one-to-one sessions with a child. She was working full-time so would be able to accommodate many more children than Elizabeth and I had ever been able to manage.

One of the first children Hilary worked with was a pretty blonde thirteen-year-old girl called Anna. She was in care and before she arrived, Hilary had been warned that in her lifetime she had been horribly abused by more than one man. As a result, she panicked when she came into contact with men. She certainly couldn't deal with being in a confined space with a man she didn't know. Obviously, this would be an ever-greater handicap as she grew up and her care workers wondered if some carefully managed one-to-one visits to Greatwood might help.

Hilary took her into the classroom for a chat first of all, and told me later that she was withdrawn but not uncommunicative. They talked about some of the horses and how Greatwood helped them, and about safety issues around the farm. Anna was wearing jeans, trainers and a hoodie, which was fine, but she had very neatly manicured nails, painted in a pale shade of pink, with tiny lacquered flowers on the tips.

'Your nails are lovely but I'm afraid they might not survive unchipped if we do any physical work,' Hilary told her with a smile.

'That's OK,' Anna said. 'I like redoing them. I've got loads of different colours.'

'Why don't we start by taking the dogs for a walk, and you'll get a chance to look round the farm and get your bearings?'

Anna crouched down to pet the dogs as soon as they bounded over and seemed relaxed when the geese wandered past as well, so she was obviously comfortable around animals. It's just one half of the human population she had a problem with. As they walked, Hilary asked her about life in care. She didn't open up much that first day but she mentioned how she hated other people barging into her room and borrowing her things, and how she was worried about what she would do in the future because she would have to leave the home at sixteen.

'They'll look after you,' Hilary soothed. 'You won't be on your own. I know it feels scary but you'll find there are systems in place.'

When they got to a field with some horses in it, Anna was perfectly confident about stroking any that came over to the fence and feeding them handfuls of grass. She didn't seem remotely nervous with our huge Thoroughbreds.

'Aren't they beautiful?' Hilary commented. 'Next week when you come back you can help to groom some horses, if you like.'

'Yes, I'd like that,' she replied shyly.

She seemed reticent when asked about school, and Hilary discovered one of the reasons for this when they got back to the classroom. She had decided that she wanted each child who came on the programme to create a kind of diary of their experiences, at whatever level of literacy they were able to manage, but when she mentioned the idea, Anna froze.

'I don't really like writing,' she whispered.

'I know you've missed a lot of school over the years, but you need to practise your writing now or it will hold you back in the future.'

'I always get the spelling wrong. I'm rubbish at spelling.'

'Well, what do you want to say? I'll write it on the whiteboard and you can copy it,' Hilary suggested.

Anna painstakingly copied out a couple of sentences about what she had seen that morning, then decorated the page with some very pretty drawings of horses, dogs, chickens and geese, so that it almost looked like a medieval illuminated manuscript. Hilary complimented her and, before she left, reminded her that the following week she should come suitably dressed for grooming the horses, in clothes that she didn't mind getting dirty.

On that first visit, they had managed to stay out of the way of any men working on the farm, but during the week, Hilary wondered how she would manage it when they went into the stables. She didn't want to ask anyone to stay out of the way because then she would have to explain why, and Anna had a right to confidentiality. She decided just to wait and see how things went on the day. If Robbie, Gary or Michael came in and Anna was upset, they'd have to move on.

The following week, Hilary smiled to see that Anna's nails were painted in a new colour scheme – aquamarine with neat black tips. They had a chat in the classroom and then Hilary took her to meet the Shetland ponies, telling her about their individual stories.

There had recently been a tragedy. I had entered Red's stable with the morning feed to find that Toffee had died in the night, standing bolt upright. Red was distraught and refused to recognise that Toffee had gone, so we had to leave the body in there for forty-eight hours to let him get used to the idea. After that, we knew we had to find another companion for Red as soon as possible, and the obvious answer was Tish.

Tish was a natural nursemaid of a pony. After Darcy Day, he had looked after several of our other horses, particularly Hamadeen and Athletic Sam, and he likes to feel useful. He's a larger-than-life character, and I'm sure he thinks he's 16.3 hands rather than just two foot tall. So with crossed fingers, we brought Tish into Red's stable shortly after Toffee's death. Red snorted a couple of times, but Tish squared off and basically told him to behave himself, and now they love each other to bits. It will probably be Tish's last nurse-maid job because he's getting on a bit, but he does it admirably.

We also had three other Shetlands at the time – Toyboy, Aaron and Poncho – but they didn't display the same caring qualities as Tish, preferring to be stabled with each other rather than with horses. Hilary took Anna to visit them, explained what they ate, how to groom them and how to muck out the barn, and then asked if Anna would like to have a go at brushing one of them. She chose Poncho, the fluffy black one, and was working away carefully when all of a sudden Edward popped his head round the barn door.

'Hello!' he boomed, smiling broadly.

'Hi, Edward,' Hilary replied casually, without looking round at Anna.

'The baker's van is here,' Edward said. 'D'you want something?'

'Not today, thanks. I brought my own lunch. Anna, do you want anything from the baker's van?'

Anna shook her head, concentrating on brushing Poncho's coat. She didn't panic, didn't burst into tears or run away, so after he left, Hilary decided to talk to her about Edward.

'He's been here for longer than anyone else except Helen and Michael, the owners. He comes two days a week and everybody loves him. You probably noticed how cheerful he is, like a ray of sunshine.'

Anna just nodded and carried on grooming. It was a start, Hilary thought. Edward hadn't come very close to her but he was a stranger, and a man, and she had managed to cope with that.

The following week, Hilary decided to take Anna over to the main stable to groom a mare called Lucky. It can be quite scary the first time you encounter a full-grown Thoroughbred up close, so Hilary hoped that one of the female staff would be around to hold her still. They got to the stable door, peered inside, and the only person in sight was Robbie. Hilary stopped and made a mental calculation. Was it too much to expect Anna to come into a stable and work in close proximity to Robbie, whom she had never met? Would it be too traumatic for her? She decided to take the risk, but be ready to curtail the session if necessary.

'Robbie, do you have a moment? Could you give us a hand with Lucky?'

'Course, no problem.'

He came over and Hilary introduced him to Anna briefly, then carried on talking to her about grooming and the brushes that should be used on the bigger horses.

'Are you ready to have a go?' she asked. As she passed a brush to Anna, she realised her hands were shaking. In fact, her whole body was trembling. It was shocking to see a child quite so scared because a man was close by, but Hilary decided not to give up just yet. She positioned herself in between Anna and Robbie, and carried on talking as if everything were normal.

'It's quite daunting the first time you're up close with these big animals,' she said. 'Some children are paralysed with fear, but I say to them, "What do you think he's going to do to you? He's not galloping around, he's not trying to bite or kick you, in fact he's just standing still enjoying being groomed." You're doing a great job, Anna. Lucky seems very contented.'

Robbie chipped in: 'She came to us with a neurological problem, poor soul, but she's a lovely character. She's got a spot right under her belly where she loves being brushed. Right there.' He reached round and touched the place.

Anna drew back quickly, as if she'd been stung, and began to breathe rapidly. There was a moment when Hilary thought she was going to have to call a halt to the session but Anna managed to control her panic and stepped forward to brush in the spot Robbie had indicated.

'You're a natural,' Robbie told her. 'This can't possibly be your first time around horses. You'd better watch out or all of the mares in here will be queuing up wanting a turn.'

'Have you been working with Fifi this morning?' Hilary asked him.

'I have indeed. She's not been ridden before,' he explained to Anna, 'and when I get on her back, she turns her head and gives me this look as if to say, "For goodness' sake, what are you playing at?" She doesn't try to throw me – at least she hasn't yet – but I wouldn't say she's accepted it by any means.' He chuckled.

Anna carried on brushing determinedly, her head down, until Lucky was gleaming all over.

'Shall we walk out to the fields now?' Hilary suggested. 'Get a bit of fresh air?'

As they walked, she told Anna something about Robbie's past. 'Before he came to Greatwood, he worked in racing. He's been doing that since he left school and he's trained lots of good horses over the years, so he's very knowledgeable. He just loves them. He's a good man.'

There was a long pause, then Anna spoke in a voice that was little more than a whisper. 'I don't like men very much.'

Hilary nodded sympathetically. 'There are some bad men in the world – you only have to watch the news to see that – but the vast majority are good. It's the same with women. There are good ones and not so good ones. The trick is learning how to judge who you can trust and who you can't, and that's something you'll get better at as you get older.'

She let a silence hang in the air, wondering if Anna wanted to say any more, but she didn't.

'You were very brave today,' Hilary told her before she left. 'Well done.' She didn't specify exactly how Anna had been brave, but the message was clear.

Having got over that first hurdle, during the next few sessions Anna gradually became more relaxed around Robbie. He was so obviously good-natured and harmless, with his light, easy banter and ready smile, that she soon felt able to ask him questions about his work in the Racing Industry, about methods of training horses, and about the personalities of some of the Thoroughbreds at Greatwood. He was a witty raconteur, always happy to chat.

Anna worked with several of the horses, but became particularly attached to Monty, which I found an interesting match. Monty was the one who took care of Sunny and Steady Eddy when they returned to us, and he was a strong character to say the least. He'd had an amazing racing career, running 104 times and coming first on eleven occasions, including prestigious races such as the Dewhurst Rockingham Stakes at York and the Hopeful Stakes.

Despite Monty's courage around other horses in the herd, he could take fright easily. One glance at an object he didn't recognise, such as a pheasant feeder, and he'd be off into the distance at the kind of lightning speeds he used to achieve on the racecourse. He could also be unpredictable. Some days he didn't want to be groomed and would try to get you out of his stable by pacing around and butting you with his nose. He wasn't being horrible; he just wasn't in the mood for being touched or fussed over.

Anna seemed to like the fact that he was a bit of a monkey. He made her laugh with his antics, and her whole face transformed, the normal guarded expression vanishing and her eyes lighting up.

She came to us for twelve sessions altogether – her nails a different colour every time – and by the end she was comfortable with all of the men around the yard.

'Can you ask Gary to show you where there's a broom?' Hilary would ask, and she'd trot over to get the broom.

'Could you nip into the office and tell Michael the farrier is here? He wanted a word with him.' She'd hurry into the office and pass on the message.

Twelve weeks was not long enough to overcome all the awful experiences Anna had had in her young life. Hilary never attempted to ask her about them directly and Anna didn't volunteer information. However, she met a few men at Greatwood whom she knew she could trust. They'd have gone out of their way to see no harm came to her, and I think that must have been obvious to her.

She took away with her some happy memories and a beautifully illustrated diary of her time at Greatwood. If that, and the ornate nail decorations, are anything to go by, she could end up in some kind of artistic career. She also took away with her a little more confidence than she'd had when she arrived. I hope I never again see anyone shaking with fear because there's a man nearby. It's one thing being nervous around our Thoroughbreds, but Robbie? Hardly.

Chapter 15

Ben and Leguard Express

Michael and I had long decided that there shouldn't be any fixed criteria for the horses that come to Greatwood. We would never turn away a horse at risk. We don't ask for a donation, don't have an age limit and don't insist on a horse passing a veterinary examination before coming to us. We either rehome horses or keep them ourselves for as long as they have a decent quality of life. Sometimes, if we have to pick up emergency cases, we need to create extra stables in any conceivable corner of the yard. On many occasions Michael has started nervously when hearing an unusual noise in the cottage, worried that perhaps I had even managed to stable a horse in the cupboard under the stairs.

We were the only racehorse charity that didn't have entry criteria, and the upshot was that we had to pick up the pieces and help with the older or more problematic horses that had nowhere else to go. Many of them had all sorts of mental and physical issues, and would be well-nigh impossible to rehome. But we believed that no healthy horse should be put to sleep, so it meant that our population was ever-increasing and our finances remained a source of stress.

I am a firm believer that horses should have a job and one of the benefits of expanding the Horse Power programme meant that the older, steadier horses would have a purpose in life, doing something worthwhile. I'm absolutely convinced that they know when they're doing good. They sense people's vulnerabilities and are extra-cautious around the weakest. I once had a very skittish horse, a complete nit-wit that was forever dancing from side to side. An elderly man with Parkinson's disease came into the yard with his daughter, looking for a horse he would be able to ride, and the moment he got on the skittish horse, it walked as carefully as if it were carrying a china teapot. All our horses are careful around the children. I've seen them twisting themselves into the most awkward, uncomfortable positions rather than shifting their weight around and risk standing on a child's toe. The whole thing was a symbiotic circle: the children helped the horses who helped the children.

Leguard Express came to us when he was nineteen. He'd been quite successful on the racecourse, with several wins on the flat and over hurdles, but he'd sustained an injury that meant he could no longer be ridden. His owner had kept him for sentimental reasons but after he died, his elderly widow could no longer cope and asked us to look after him. It was obvious we couldn't rehome him because he couldn't be ridden but we felt we had to take him to help the widow, who was still in the depths of mourning over her husband's death. We certainly didn't think we should add to her grief by suggesting that her only option was to put Leguard down. We picked him up, brought him to Greatwood and, after a day's acclimatisation, we let him out into the field where we kept our other 'old boys', Sunny, Eddy and Monty.

At first Leguard seemed shy and retiring. It took us a while to realise that he was wound up like a coiled spring, constantly on his guard against all the strange new sights, horses and people he was encountering. To me he just seemed withdrawn and I found it unusually hard to get any sense of his character. He threw a bit of a paddy if we had to bring him in to see the farrier or the vet, but so did lots of the others. It was difficult to get to the bottom of this dark bay gelding, with just a few white hairs between his eyes.

After he'd been with us for about three months, I walked out one morning to do a field check and, much to my astonishment, Leguard trotted over to say hello. He'd never done that before so I made a huge fuss of him. This was really the first bit of interest he had shown in anyone since his arrival. A few days later when I went by I saw him play-fighting with Monty, both of them circling and rearing up, having a rare old time. A new character was emerging. It transpired that the true Leguard Express was a lively, affectionate, calm and loving horse. It had taken him a few months to let us see this side because of the stress of the move – and probably because he missed his old owner as well – but when it emerged it was lovely to watch.

I realised that Leguard would be a good horse to work with visiting children, because he was very gentle, patient enough to stand still while he was being groomed, and stable enough not to panic at sudden movements or noises. I'd found that the children were always more impressed by horses who had won lots of races and Leguard certainly came into that category. Besides, it would be good for him to have a role on the farm. I knew from experience that it would give him a sense of purpose and pride to be able to perform a role.

Just after Leguard's arrival, Hilary had a challenge when a boy called Ben arrived as part of a mixed group from a mainstream school.

'What a dump!' she heard him exclaiming as he was led into the classroom.

'Good morning. My name's Hilary,' she said by way of introduction to the group, and noted their expressions of surprise. They were obviously used to more formality from their teachers, but she liked to be on first-name terms. 'Please would you all write your names on the badges in front of you and stick them on so that I know who you are?'

She wandered round looking over their shoulders as they completed the task, trying to memorise the names. When she got to Ben, she saw that he had written 'Osama bin Laden' on his sticker. She decided to ignore it for now, even when all the children round about began sniggering at his bravado. It was interesting that he had spelled it correctly, she mused. He was a bright little Jack the lad. Looking at the register, she worked out his real name.

As she talked through safety issues on the farm, Ben was full of smart-alec comments delivered under his breath.

'Why shouldn't we leave gates open? Might make things a bit more fun round here ...' 'You won't catch me shovelling any shit ...'

Still, Hilary let such remarks pass. She explained about the need not to shriek or yell because the rescue horses could be very timid, and showed PowerPoint presentations of some of the Thoroughbreds they would meet, while explaining their histories.

'If we all yell together, it might make them throw off their riders,' Ben snickered to his neighbours. 'Who wants to try?'

Hilary continued: 'I've written the timetable for your visit on the board here. In a minute I'll be taking you to meet some of the horses, but would you rather stay here, Ben?'

'It's Osama to you.'

'Ben, you're holding up the rest of the group who all want to get out and see the horses. It's your choice. Do you want to come with us or not?'

'OK,' he shrugged. 'Why not?'

'I've explained the rules and anyone who doesn't follow them will have to come back and work here in the classroom. We can't take any risks with your safety.'

Ben was nudging and jostling his friends as they headed out to the yard, but as soon as they got into the stable there was a collective sharp intake of breath. The sheer size of the animals never fails to impress children, and they started with one of the most impressive horses we've ever had.

'This is Deano's Beano,' Hilary said, and began to tell them his story.

Deano's was a hurdler with an excellent record of eleven major wins under his belt. He's still recognised as one of racing's top-staying hurdlers. Tony McCoy partnered him, but he had to earn his fee on many occasions because Deano's had a mind of his own and would only race if he felt like it. Despite that, Tony and trainer Martin Pipe still reckon he's their firm favourite of all the horses they've trained. When he retired in 2004, Deano's was gifted to Greatwood, probably because they thought we would be able to deal with his quirky nature better than most.

There were all sorts of articles in the press at the time praising his amazing career, and I was a little concerned by the responsibility of caring for such a popular and enigmatic animal. I began to worry that something might go wrong and there would be headlines reading 'Deano's Meets Early Death at Greatwood'. He had come to us in impeccable condition, a picture of health. How could I keep him safe?

At first I tried putting him in with the ponies but he didn't seem interested in them. There was something about him that made me pretty sure he would be useless in a herd. He was too arrogant and self-important. He was bound to get into a scrap with another horse and once that happened he would never be the one to back down

As it happened, though, we had just taken on a small dark bay called Paul Cass. Paul was about as unlike Deano's Beano as you could possibly imagine; in his only race at Catterick he had come fifteenth out of fifteen. Paul had a neurological problem that meant he was uncomfortable under saddle, so we had retired him to our sanctuary. Was there a chance he would get on with Deano's?

When we introduced them, Deano's roared and Paul retreated, which was exactly the result we wanted. If Paul had retaliated, it would have turned into full-scale war. We left them in a stable for a few days to get used to each other then turned them out. It was nerve-racking to witness Deano's galloping up the field at full tilt, and I had visions of all kinds of accidents in my mind, but in fact he quickly calmed down. He and Paul soon became fast friends.

We realised Deano's was bound for the sanctuary as well after Sue tried to ride him and he steadfastly refused. After all, the great Tony McCoy had trouble on one notorious occasion at Cheltenham when Deano's simply refused to start. If he found it difficult, it didn't give us much of a chance. So it was decided that Deano's Beano would stay with us for life.

He has a compelling presence, an aristocratic air and big intelligent eyes. Deano's always appears superior, as if he is looking down on us mere human beings. Sue laughs about what she calls his 'signature strut' as he walks around looking imperiously down his nose at his many admirers. He has now become Greatwood's flagship horse and we are quite often invited to events in recognition of his illustrious career on the racecourse.

Hilary noticed that while she was talking about Deano's, Ben had shut up and was listening intently to every word, especially the bit about his friendship with Paul Cass, who had never won a race in his life. 'At Greatwood it's not about winning or being the best,' she said. 'Everyone has a place, and we love Paul because he keeps Deano's calm and happy.'

They have the odd scrap when Deano's insists on chasing Paul about and grabbing his rug and tail with his teeth until Paul finally retaliates with a swift left hook. But on an average day, they normally breakfast together then head off to a shady corner for a snooze. 'You're lucky they're awake today,' Hilary told the group. 'Many's the time I've brought visiting children here to find them out for the count and nothing we could do would rouse them.'

She glanced round at Ben to see if he would take this as a challenge, but he was quiet and thoughtful-looking – quite a different child from the one in the classroom. Deano's is such a commanding presence that he often strikes the children dumb. Ben didn't utter another peep as they walked round meeting a few more horses, but when they headed back to the classroom for a snack break, all the old behaviour re-emerged.

Hilary had introduced the snack break as a time when the children could interact with each other and discuss what they had seen. She wanted them to demonstrate good manners, passing round a plate of cake or biscuits, and pouring drinks for each other. First of all, Ben grabbed the whole plate of cake – 'I'm 'aving that' – then he spilled his juice on the floor in a manner that Hilary suspected was deliberate. She got him a mop but his exaggerated, clown-like mopping motions merely spread the wet patch around. He was infuriating, but she had a cunning plan for the next part of the morning, when she would take the children on a tour of the farm.

Earlier on in the year Michael had taken on a yellow Labrador puppy called Hannah. At only six months old, she was full of exuberance, prone to jumping up and not yet very good at walking on the lead.

'Ben, could you walk Hannah for us? Make sure she doesn't eat anything she finds on the ground and don't let her too close to any other animals.'

Hilary handed over the lead and Ben found himself in charge of a leaping, twisting, yapping bundle of unchannelled energy. It took all his strength and focus to keep control of her as they toured the paths round the perimeter of the farm, and he had no time for sarky comments or joshing with his classmates. All she could hear was, 'Stop it, Hannah. Down, girl. Leave that alone.' She chuckled. He was getting a taste of his own medicine.

As they walked back to the classroom for a round-up before they left, she told them that the following week they would be cleaning out the goats' and hens' sheds.

'They're just using us as cheap labour,' Ben commented to his neighbours, but none of them responded. His antics weren't impressing anyone any more. While they were washing their hands after coming in from the yard he'd turned and splashed water at the others, trying to start a full-scale water fight, but they just grumbled at him to 'grow up'. Hilary stood back, ready to intervene if it got out of hand, but she was pleased to let his peers put him in his place rather than having to do so herself.

Already she could see that Ben's behaviour masked a deep-seated insecurity and during the week she put a lot of thought into how she could work with him to help him get the most from his time at Greatwood. She called a teacher at Ben's school and asked about his background.

'There are domestic violence issues at home,' she was told. 'He sometimes comes to school with black eyes and a cut lip. We think it happens when he's been trying to protect his mum from his dad but if we ask he just says, "Walked into a door, Miss." We're struggling to know what to do with him because he's bright but he just won't apply himself and do the work. He says he can't see the point of learning, and he's always in trouble for fighting with his classmates. But throwing a punch is the main behaviour he sees at home. There's no decent role model for him.'

Acting up and fighting was his defence mechanism to stop anyone getting close. He was a child who saw only bad in other people and didn't expect much from the world. Hilary was encouraged that he had seemed to be interested in the animals, though. She decided that when he came back, she would give him responsibility for looking after some more animals to see how he got on.

On the second visit, once again Ben acted up in the classroom. Hilary had pointedly left out a new badge for him to write his name on and this time he wrote 'Tony Blair'. He interrupted while she was talking, whispered to his neighbours and couldn't stop fidgeting.

'Ben, I am about to send you into a shed with three boisterous goats and you won't have a clue what to do with them because you are not listening to the instructions,' she said. 'If you carry on like this I won't ever be able to let you work with the horses, because it could be dangerous if you don't know what you're doing.'

He muttered something she couldn't catch but then settled down a bit. Once out in the yard, Hilary threw him in at the deep end. It had worked when she'd put him in charge of Hannah; what he needed was a challenge to engage him.

'OK, Ben, there's the goat shed. In you go. They need their beds cleaned out, their water refreshed and the hay manger filled.'

Our goats, Ted, Bill and Reg, bounded over and Ben looked nervous. He waited until a couple of the other children had gone over to stroke them before deciding it must be safe to copy their example. Hilary took pity on him and repeated the instructions she'd given in the classroom.

'Remember, only throw out the dirty old straw. We're a charity and can't afford waste. Scrub the feed buckets carefully so they don't get ill, and make sure the water is fresh and clean.'

Ben opened the gate and went into the shed with a couple of the others, and he worked hard for the next hour. Hilary kept glancing over and she didn't once see him stop for a rest or wind up the other children.

When she came back to inspect the work, she was impressed at how neat and clean it was. 'This looks perfect to me. There's nothing at all I would criticise in here.'

Ben had a question. 'Who's that horse there?' he asked. 'It kept poking its head over to watch.'

'That's Leguard Express,' Hilary told him, and explained a bit about his background. 'Do you like him?'

'He's OK,' Ben shrugged, trying to be offhand but not succeeding.

'You can groom him next week if you like,' she smiled, and Ben's normally surly expression broke into a huge grin.

The following week, Hilary knew she was making headway when he wrote 'Ben' on the name badge she left out. He listened carefully in the classroom as she explained about the different tools used for grooming and demonstrated the basic techniques, and then he followed the group out to the yard.

Hilary had asked Robbie to hold Leguard Express while Ben groomed him. As Ben worked, Robbie began chatting away about Leguard's racing career, and then he told him a little about his own career in the racing world. Ben's eyes lit up when he realised he was in the company of a successful professional horseman. How impressive was that?

'You're doing a grand job there,' Robbie said as Ben smoothed down Leguard's coat. 'Look, he's closed his eyes. That's a compliment. It means you've relaxed him.'

Ben was obviously falling for Leguard but he was also seriously impressed by Robbie. At every visit from then on, he sought out Robbie to ask him yet more questions about racing, and Robbie was always happy to answer. He was particularly keen on asking questions about how to back youngsters, and wanted to know how often Robbie had been thrown off ('Lots!'), how long it took ('It varies from horse to horse') and whether there had ever been a horse he just couldn't train ('Not yet, but there's bound to be one some day').

Ben stood and watched one morning as Robbie rode a new horse round and round our training ring, patting its neck and talking softly to reassure it. Suddenly it occurred to Hilary that this could be the first time Ben had ever seen a man being gentle and affectionate. Robbie was strong and highly respected in his career and as such he was the perfect role model for an impressionable young boy who saw quite a different example at home. If only Ben could model himself on Robbie rather than his violent father.

To Ben's great delight, Leguard began to recognise him when he arrived and to trot over for a pat, whether he was in a field or in the stable. He had a friend. Leguard had been stressed and watchful when he arrived at Greatwood but once he relaxed he'd shown a lovely nature, and Ben was similar. When he stopped acting out, you could see there was a really nice boy in there.

Hilary spoke to Ben's teacher again just before his last session at Greatwood. 'It's made a real difference,' the teacher said. 'None of us can believe it but he's started putting his hand up and answering questions in class, and his work has improved by leaps and bounds. He hasn't started a fight for at least three weeks, and that's a record for him.'

As with so many other troubled young people that pass through our care, we've had no feedback about how Ben is doing now, but I hope he's been able to build on what he learned in his weeks here and find more role models, more tasks that hold his attention and more people to love.

Chapter 16

Mary and Tim

Michael had long been keen on offering children some sort of qualification that they could work for, so that they left Greatwood feeling a real sense of achievement, and Hilary was keen to help take this idea to the next stage. They decided that anyone completing the basic six-week Horse Power course would be awarded a certificate, but Hilary also designed a ten-week course for children aged fourteen and over, called 'Developing Confidence Through Working with Animals', and she managed to achieve accreditation. There were a number of challenges they would have to complete but the certificate they'd receive at the end would be a nationally recognised qualification that could help them in their future careers.

There would be different parts of the course, and they would have to pass each one to get the certificate. The first part was about personal safety and taking responsibility for the safety of others; the next was about learning to care for a range of different animals; and finally they would learn about reading body language in animals and in human beings. A lot of the time they would be expected to do hard physical work and deal directly with the Thoroughbreds, although always under supervision.

We were delighted when Hilary's course was accredited. It was the vision Michael and I had had some time earlier but it needed her energy and experience to make it happen. As soon as it was in place, and Hilary had explained to schools about what we could offer, there was a renewed rush of applications to come to Greatwood so children could do our course.

Amongst one of the first groups to come after the award scheme started was a girl called Mary, a stroppy teenager with attitude who had twice been excluded from school for disruptive behaviour. She had been in trouble with the police on a few occasions for attacking her brother. Her home life was obviously very unhappy and school wasn't much better. She had been known to take a swing at her classmates and was always back-chatting the teachers. They'd more or less given up on her. Everyone had. That's why her teachers were astonished when she said she wanted to come to Greatwood and do the course. They stared at her open-mouthed. She'd never shown any interest in animals before. She hadn't been interested in learning, full stop.

When Hilary first met Mary, she didn't think she had the right attitude to make it through the course. Her chest was spilling out of a seriously low-cut top, her jeans were so tight she could barely walk, and she chewed gum incessantly, with an audible chomping sound. She slumped down in the classroom and pulled a can of Red Bull from her bag.

Hilary knew it was an energy drink and decided the last thing she wanted was for Mary to be wired on caffeine. 'I'm afraid you can't drink that here,' she said. 'We've got some squash, or we can make a cup of tea or hot chocolate at break time.'

With a loud sigh, Mary put the can back in her bag. Another girl, Cheryl, whispered something to her and they both giggled loudly. Hilary ignored them and started on the safety talk, aware that they were still whispering and gesticulating to each other behind her back.

Cheryl came from a different school so they hadn't met before, but she latched on to Mary that first morning, seeing her as the perfect partner in crime. Cheryl was a big girl with a history of violence, and the teaching assistant who had accompanied the children from her school seemed nervous of her. 'This could get interesting if it all kicks off,' Hilary thought to herself warily.

Out in the yard, as she showed them around, Hilary asked Mary to go and get a particular brush from the storeroom. She'd already explained about the different types of brush and was testing to see whether Mary had been listening.

'Nah, get it yourself,' Mary muttered, and Cheryl burst into fits of laughter, as if it were the cleverest thing she'd ever heard.

Hilary narrowed her eyes, but decided to send another pupil for the brush rather than have a head-on confrontation. Next, she set them all tasks – simple ones for the first day, such as sweeping the yard and cleaning tackle. She tried to separate Mary and Cheryl, sending them to opposite ends of the yard, but when she looked round Cheryl had dragged her saddle across and was half-heartedly rubbing it while chatting to Mary. It looked as though they were going to be bonded at the hip.

Both girls were nervous around the horses, standing well back and refusing to stroke them, covering up their nerves with supercilious commentary. When it was time to do some mucking out, Hilary thought Mary would turn her nose up at it because it would mean getting dirty and smelly, but she picked up a shovel and did her bit.

Cheryl, on the other hand, shrieked, 'That's disgusting!' while wafting her hand in front of her face. 'I can't do that, Miss. I'd be sick.'

Hilary shrugged. They either completed the course or they didn't – and if they didn't, they wouldn't get a certificate. That's all there was to it. They could spend their time chatting and chewing gum in the yard if they so chose. She wasn't sure whether Mary and Cheryl would even come back the following week, but when the buses from their respective schools pulled up, there they both were. She sighed.

During that second week, the children got to try grooming the horses. Mary and Cheryl stood well back, but Hilary could see that Mary was interested.

'I like that one with the blond hair,' she said, pointing at Tim. 'Look, there are lots of different shades of blond in it, as if he's had highlights. Wish I could get mine to go like that!'

'Come and meet him,' Hilary suggested.

Mary stepped forward tentatively and Hilary shoved a brush in her hand. 'Remember what I told you. Brush in the direction of the hair.' She stepped away and left Mary to it and when she looked back, she saw that it was working. She was engrossed in the task and had completely overcome her nervousness.

Mary soon become enamoured of Tim, who she thought was an especially pretty horse. Each week, she combed his mane until it was smooth and tangle-free. If we'd let her I'm sure she'd have tried out different hair-styles on him. It wasn't a match based on similar person-alities or life experiences, as we'd had between other children and horses; in this case, it was more about hair-dressing. However, when she wasn't with Tim, Mary still hung around with Cheryl, the two of them playing at being the bad girls of the group. It wasn't cool to be seen to work hard; it wasn't cool to show enthusiasm.

Each week on the course, Hilary gave the pupils slightly more responsibility for the animals. In weeks two and three, she stood by and helped them in their tasks, but by weeks four and five she was beginning to hold back and it was up to them to get the work done. It was during week five that she saw a real change come over Mary. She was in the goats' enclosure, trying to sort out their straw, and Cheryl was leaning against the fence chatting to her. Hilary wandered past and looked in without a word, and as she walked away, she heard Mary say, 'I've got to get on now. Why don't you go and do your own stuff?'

Hilary paused round the corner to eavesdrop on the rest of their conversation.

'Who cares about the bloody animals? It's just a way of getting a morning off school, ain't it?' Cheryl replied.

'I want to get the certificate,' Mary said. 'We're here so we might as well give it a go. We're halfway through the course already and there's loads still to learn.'

'Why do you want a stupid bit of paper? You gone soft in the head?'

'I just want it, that's all.'

Cheryl stomped off in a huff and Mary carried on mucking out with renewed vigour.

Hilary was delighted that Mary had decided to apply herself to the course, although she suspected it was largely to do with Tim. His gentle, placid character had somehow steadied Mary and made her calm down.

By weeks six to eight of the course, Hilary expected the group to work as a team, organising who was responsible for each task. They had to decide the tools they needed, do the work, clean the tools and put them away, then when they'd finished they would go and find Hilary, and ask her to check what they'd done. As well as animal care, they were learning a sense of personal responsibility.

By this stage, Mary was having little to do with Cheryl. There was no more standing around whispering and sniggering. She'd become a different person. She started thinking about the work and figuring out for herself what needed to be done. She was proud when she could remember something that everyone else had forgotten. At break times, she chatted with the others about the horses instead of sitting at the back chewing gum and making sarky comments under her breath.

'Can anyone tell me what they've observed about horses' body language?' Hilary asked during the break time in week eight.

'It's their ears, innit? If they're flat back, it means they're not happy, and if they are perked up they're happy,' one boy commented.

Mary chipped in: 'Tim doesn't like it if I look him in the eyes. Why is that?'

'Why do you think?' Hilary asked. 'What does it mean to you if someone looks you straight in the eyes?'

'They're trying to stare me out 'cos they want a fight.'

'Maybe that's what Tim feels. It's a sign of dominance and it scares him. It's less threatening for animals – and for people – if you keep your gaze moving around rather than staring straight at them.'

'Unless you fancy them,' Cheryl retorted from the back of the room, but everyone ignored her. In fact, she had settled down as well after she realised that Mary was no longer a willing accomplice, and her work was coming on nicely, even if she still displayed a bit of bravado from time to time.

In week ten, Hilary was delighted to be able to tell Mary, Cheryl and the rest of the group that they had all passed the course. We were having an open day a couple of weeks later and champion jockey Mick Fitzgerald had agreed to come and present the certificates to the children who had passed so far.

'I can't do that,' Mary cried. 'I'm not getting up on a stage with lots of people watching. I'd be terrified. Can't you just give me mine separately?'

'Everyone else is doing it,' Hilary explained. 'You'd be missing out if you didn't. Just take a deep breath and put one foot in front of the other. Remember that you used to be scared of the horses when you first came here. You got over that, didn't you?'

'But what if I trip and fall flat on my face?'

'If you do you'll just have to get up and carry on.'

Hilary felt strongly that Mary should force herself to go through with the presentation in recognition of what she had achieved, and on the day she managed it, albeit bright red in the face. She even managed to pose for the official photographs.

Mary's mum came up to have a quiet word with Hilary. 'She's much better at home since she's been coming here. Much less angry. She can still be difficult but she's happier than she used to be. She wants to know if she can come back and do the Level Two certificate.'

'We don't do a Level Two course yet,' Hilary told her, 'but maybe we should think about it.'

She noticed Cheryl standing around on her own, clutching her certificate. 'Is there no family here with you today?' Hilary asked.

'Nah, they weren't interested,' Cheryl replied, and a hurt look flickered across her face.

'You've done well,' Hilary told her. 'Remember that. Whatever you set your mind to, you can achieve.'

'Yeah, whatever,' she said, before she ambled off to the minibus that was going to take her home again.

Mary and Cheryl's group were a success story for Greatwood, and so were all the groups that came to do our new course – all, that is, except one. We got a call from the team leader of a group of inner-city kids who were on a countryside holiday, asking if she could bring some of them along. Hilary said that the biggest group she could accept was six, and a date was agreed.

On the morning in question, a bus pulled up and fifteen children jumped out along with two teachers who, it transpired, didn't even know the children. They'd just been roped in for some freelance work.

The children were wearing wholly unsuitable clothes and shoes for a farm visit: high heels and short skirts on the girls, while the boys had those trousers that are hanging down their bottoms so their underpants are exposed.

Hilary took a deep breath and herded them all into the classroom but they made it quite clear from their attitude that they weren't going to cooperate.

'I don't like animals, Miss. What else you got here?'

'Is there a caff? Where can we get a Coke?'

She persevered in running through the safety talk, and then took them out to meet some horses, hoping that they'd experience the usual sense of awe at the first sight of our Thoroughbreds. Some of them were hooked, but the others stood at the back, chatting amongst themselves and complaining that they were bored. Mabel the dog jumped up at one girl and she shrieked that she was going to sue if her tights got ripped.

Hilary attempted to take them on a tour of the farm but it had been raining heavily the day before and their shoes just weren't up to the muddy areas. It was sad that the ones who were genuinely interested shouldn't be allowed to get the benefit of the whole experience but there weren't enough staff to split them into two separate groups. She took them back to the yard to meet the goats, the Shetland ponies, the chickens and the geese, but she didn't have their full attention and eventually called it a day.

Hilary spoke on the phone to the team leader and asked if only the children who were interested could be sent along the following week, and she requested a ratio of at least one teacher to every six children. When the bus turned up, however, it was the same bored group of fifteen. Hilary asked who would like to have a go at grooming the horses and only six said that they would. One girl then dropped out when she learned she would have to wear a hard hat, which would make her hairstyle go flat. It was a disaster, and after that second visit, Hilary phoned and told them not to come back. If someone genuinely isn't interested in animals, there's little we can do to convert them.

This was a one-off, though. In all the years we've been running the Horse Power course, it's the only time we've had to ask a group not to come back. Most children become horse-mad and count the days until they can return to us, and I suspect that a huge majority of those achieving our certificate go on to look for some kind of career working with animals. A life-long passion has been sparked.

Chapter 17

The Importance of Food

Riding ponies is a normal country pursuit because there are fields and stables where they can be kept. It's expensive to keep your own pony if you live in a town, though, and the cost of lessons (£25 an hour at the very least) mounts up rapidly. I was unbelievably lucky to be a farmer's daughter and have horses at home that I could ride in my free time. I have always been surrounded by animals and simply couldn't envisage a life without them.

If children are interested in horses but their parents can't afford lessons, I always suggest that they turn up at their local stables or farm as a volunteer. Most places will be happy to have an extra pair of hands when mucking out and chances are you'll get a ride every now and then.

Sadly, we can't let children ride the horses at Greatwood. Even the most even-tempered racehorses can be too unpredictable for small, inexperienced children to learn to ride on. This is explained to everyone before they come here, but there are always some who complain and try to change our minds. 'Aw, please, Miss. What's the point if we can't have a ride?'

I always say to them that grooming horses can be an immensely satisfying experience, especially if you have the time to relax and enjoy it. They will let you know the areas that require special attention, and the parts of their body that they can't reach and would love you to scratch. Most horses particularly enjoy their heads being brushed, providing that you do it carefully and gently. It's wonderful to see a horse lower its head so that a child can reach it. Sometimes it will even curl its head around the child almost like a cuddle. The smell and closeness of the horse, the child's concentration on its coat, making sure that the hair is smooth and lying in the right direction, together with the obvious enjoyment of both participants, is a wonderful experience. It's as if horse and child become one for a brief while. I think this tactile experience is responsible for what we call the 'Greatwood effect' – the sense of calm contentment that seems to come over most of our visitors sooner or later.

Some of the children who come to Greatwood get under your skin more than others, for different reasons. With me, it's not the best-behaved, or the most troubled. There's no rhyme or reason to it, but I knew as soon as I saw Tommy that I wanted him to thrive here. He was only eight years old and what struck me most was how unhealthy he looked. He had a sallow, olive complexion, great dark shadows under his eyes, and he was just skin and bones. Small for his age, he looked malnourished to me, and there was something haunted about his expression.

What he lacked in pallor, however, he made up for in energy, because Tommy never stopped talking.

'It bloody stinks here,' he said as soon as he got out of the car into the yard. 'Is that poo?'

Hilary put her foot down straight away. 'We don't swear here, Tommy. If you want to swear I'm afraid you'll have to go back to school.'

He looked surprised but backed down. 'Sorry, Miss. It just slipped out.'

'Call me Hilary,' she said, before leading him into the classroom for his introductory session.

Tommy was a referral from a primary school. They were close to excluding him because his behaviour was so disruptive. He talked in class, was verbally abusive to teachers and classmates alike, and refused to do anything he was asked to do. When challenged, he would fly into a rage and throw things around the classroom. The school didn't want to exclude him but he was disturbing the others and they were running out of patience. He was sent to Greatwood on his own to see if it would make any difference to him and also, I'm sure, because the long-suffering staff wanted to give themselves a few hours of peace a week.

Right from the start, he began testing Hilary to see how much he could get away with. He knocked a pencil case onto the classroom floor and when she asked him to pick it up he refused.

'Tommy, if you want to meet the animals I have to be convinced that you will behave yourself around them. You have a choice. If you won't do what I say then we'll just sit in the classroom until the car comes to pick you up again.'

Grumbling, he bent down and picked up the case, and banged it hard on the desk. 'I've got animals of me own anyway,' he said. 'Lots of them.'

'Have you? What have you got?'

'We've got two ponies, three dogs, six cats and a hamster. The hamster is me little sister's. We've got a really big house so there's lots of room but it gets a bit mad at times.'

Hilary didn't believe a word of it. She'd come across this before. Children who have a difficult home life often invent fantasy lives in which they live in palaces and have unlimited toys and sweets and pets. 'That's nice,' she said, and carried on with the lesson.

Out in the yard, Tommy was cocky and swaggering, but when Robbie led Deano's Beano past he ducked right back out of the way, obviously scared. 'Whoah, he's a big one!'

Hilary led him around, telling him the story of each horse in the stables, and he kept up his own running

commentary. 'I bet he's fast. His legs are really long.'
'What's that one's name? He's got funny eyes.'

When they went back to the classroom for a snack break, Tommy was chatting away with excitement in a way that Hilary found quite charming. Here was another little child who just needed to have his attention engaged for him to behave perfectly well. Unfortunately, no school can afford the kind of one-on-one care it would require.

She brought out a packet of biscuits, poured some juice and before she had even sat down, Tommy reached across and grabbed a handful of biscuits.

'No,' Hilary rebuked. 'That's not the way we do things here. We don't grab biscuits. You should have offered them to me first.'

He already had a whole biscuit in his mouth and his cheeks were bulging with the effort of chewing. 'Take one if you want,' he said, the words virtually incomprehensible.

'You must be hungry,' Hilary commented, and he nodded. As soon as he swallowed one biscuit, he pushed the next into his mouth and as she watched, a thought occurred to her.

'Did you have any breakfast this morning?' she asked, and he shook his head.

'My mum forgot,' he said, spitting soggy biscuit crumbs into the air. He reached for another. She decided to let him eat as many as he wanted.

'What's your favourite dinner?' she asked. 'What's the meal you like the most?'

'Chips and crisps,' he said. 'With lots of salt and vinegar.'

'What about vegetables?'

'Nah, don't like them. They're rubbish.'

'Do you like meat or fish?'

'Yeah,' he said doubtfully. 'I had a Big Mac once and we got a free toy.'

Hilary wished she could bring him straight over to our cottage for a bowl of home-made vegetable soup and a salad. Suddenly the pasty pallor and skinny frame made sense. If the boy was malnourished, that would explain his poor attention span as well. She decided to ask the school to talk to his mother, although she wasn't sure what good it would do if they didn't have the money for decent food. Maybe he could at least have a free school lunch to get some vitamins into his system.

As they walked round the farm, they chatted all the way. Hilary asked more about his life at home and realised it was chaotic. There was no regular bedtime, meals were an ad hoc affair and he was often left without a babysitter when his mum went out with one of her boyfriends. He was right in the middle of a big family, with older siblings who had left home, and two younger ones who were still babies, but he was isolated with no natural allies, and in many ways he'd been forced to become an adult too early. He didn't get much attention at home so when he got to school he misbehaved and got himself noticed that way.

'Did you know that you are on your last chance with the school before you get excluded?' Hilary asked.

He shrugged. 'So what? There's plenty more schools in the world – worst luck.'

Hilary explained that the next place he ended up might not be as good, and that an exclusion would stay on his record. He kicked a tuft of soil and grass up into the air. 'Who cares anyway? It's only bloody school,' he shouted, then ran off down the path as fast as he could.

One minute he was well behaved and good company, and the next he was swearing, refusing to do as he was told and running off. Hilary had told him very clearly that he must never run off on the farm.

'Right!' she thought. 'A different tactic is called for.'

She knew how difficult it is to catch Toyboy and she decided to test Tommy, to let him see what it's like trying to deal with someone who runs off all the time. Toyboy was in the paddock with Aaron and Poncho, so she fetched some head collars from the yard. Tommy was hanging around by the stable door waiting to see how she would react to his disobedience.

'Could you come and help me catch the Shetland ponies?' she asked. 'Here. Take a head collar.'

She marched off, leaving him to follow. When they got to the paddock, she went in first. 'Watch carefully what I do,' she instructed, 'because it will be your turn next.'

She walked up to Poncho, slipped a head collar over his head and led him to the gate. Then she turned and did the same with Aaron.

'Did you see that? Now you go and fetch Toyboy.'

Tommy picked up a head collar and marched confidently into the field. How hard could it be? But Toyboy ducked and dived, and every time Tommy got close to him he'd sprint away.

'Hurry up!' Hilary called. 'I've done the first two ponies. I'm waiting for you.'

Tommy was becoming red in the face with the effort but he couldn't for the life of him catch Toyboy and eventually he flung the head collar to the ground in a fit of temper.

'Isn't it irritating when someone won't do something really simple that you want them to do?' Hilary asked pointedly.

She could see he'd got the message, but she hammered it home. 'Because Toyboy wasted your time like that, there's not much time left to groom the horses.' Tommy had told her he was looking forward to grooming, so that was a real disappointment for him.

Would he take the message on board? Sometimes he did, and sometimes he didn't. Throughout the twelve weekly sessions that Tommy had with Hilary, he'd switch from being cooperative to being disobedient again, one minute full of childish enthusiasm for the horses and the next throwing brushes to the ground and storming off.

'At least he's got a bit more colour in his cheeks than when he arrived,' Hilary commented as we waved good-bye to him after the last session.

'Do you think he'll get his act together and manage to stay in school?' I asked.

She pursed her lips and shook her head. 'Doubt it somehow.'

And she was right. The next time we got news of Tommy, he'd been moved to a special school for children with behavioural problems. Maybe someone there will be able to set him on the straight and narrow. With any luck, they will at least make sure he gets a decent meal every day.

In the early years of Greatwood, I visited our rehomed horses at least once a year to make sure they were thriving. As the years went by, I decided it was no longer necessary to keep going back so regularly to carers who had been looking after their horse successfully for years and years, but I might still pop in if we were in the area. Sometimes people's circumstances change and they can no longer afford vets' bills, so they don't call out a vet when they should do. Sometimes they might hear about a new fad in horse care and jump on a bandwagon that is not necessarily beneficial for the horse.

By keeping an eye on them from time to time, I can make sure that the horses remain well-nourished, healthy and happy. If there's a problem, very occasionally I've had to bring a horse back to Greatwood so that we can care for it here. Looking at Tommy, I wished we could do home visits to his house, taking along a big basket full of vegetables and a cookbook. It seemed wrong to me that we were able to take better care of the horses that passed through our hands than the children, but that's just how it was.

Chapter 18

School Phobia

Before Hilary agrees to take on a new child or school group, she has a conversation with their teacher or social worker to learn a little about their backgrounds and any special needs they might have. This is usually just a formality, but when she heard about all the problems a boy called Simon suffered from, she nearly said no, she couldn't take him. There was such a long list of issues that he sounded as though he would be difficult to handle and might not get much from the experience anyway.

Simon had a very troubled background with a horrendous catalogue of physical and emotional abuse. You'd think he would want to get out of the house but instead he hated school and used to have to be dragged out kicking and screaming each morning, with his fingers gripping the front-door frame until he was wrenched away. In the classroom he had very low self-esteem. He was dyslexic, had been diagnosed with attention deficit hyperactivity disorder, and was prone to incredibly high levels of anxiety. He felt different from the other children and was super-vigilant, constantly on the lookout for reactions from others that would confirm his difference, which made him very stressed. He had been excluded from school and the local authorities were trying to find him another place.

'I really don't know …' Hilary hesitated, having visions of her chasing him round the farm. It wasn't a safe environment for a young child (Simon was only ten) to be unsupervised.

'Please!' urged the woman from the local authority. 'We feel strongly that he will respond to a place where he is asked to do physical rather than mental tasks, and he desperately needs something to boost his self-esteem.'

'Oh, all right then,' Hilary agreed – and she was glad she had because the little boy who got out of the car and came across the yard bore little resemblance to the child who'd been described to her. He was nervous and unsure of himself, but so were most kids when they arrived. When Hilary took him round to introduce him to the animals, he loved the dogs and the goats, but was less keen on the horses – all except one. Steady Eddy.

Eddy is a very elderly horse – thirty years old now – and has worn away his front teeth. He has to eat a mush that we prepare for his meals and it's best not to go near him when he's eating because he slurps and guzzles and sprays food all around him, ending up with it all over his face right up to his eyes. Simon was tickled by the way his tongue tended to hang out his mouth.

'Look, he's sticking his tongue out!' he chuckled. The insubordination of this amused him, but in general he found the rest of the horses too big and scary. What he loved best on that first visit was feeding the chickens. He liked the way they clucked and strutted around, and he asked Hilary lots of questions about their care.

Picking up on his interest in the chickens, Hilary suggested that the following week they might build a nesting box for wild birds and put it in a secluded area of the farm. They could then check it from time to time and see if it was being used. Simon loved that idea so much he clapped his hands and gave a little skip.

After he left, Hilary scratched her head. Was this child really supposed to have ADHD? He wasn't showing any symptoms at all. He'd been attentive and responsive, and had behaved impeccably throughout the visit. It was as if there had been a bureaucratic mix-up and she had been sent a different child from the one who'd been described on the phone.

The night before Simon's second visit, Hilary suddenly remembered her promise about the nesting box. Fortunately her father made nesting boxes in his spare time, so she drove to his house and persuaded him to part with one. They dismantled it so it formed a kind of nest-box kit and when Simon arrived she gave him the pieces, along with a hammer and some little nails. He sat down on the concrete surface of the yard, happy as a sandboy despite the fact that it wasn't a very warm day, and he built himself a perfect little nesting box. All the edges were neatly fixed and every angle was accurate.

Next they had to decide where to put it. It was the right size for robins, so as they walked round the farm they discussed what robins liked and didn't like. They tried one tree after another until they finally found a place that seemed perfect and fixed it up. From then on, they went to check on the box every week. Unbeknown to Simon, Hilary often sneaked up beforehand and put in a piece of straw or moved the contents around a bit so that he would think it was in use. But before long she didn't have to bother, because it was.

Hilary realised that Simon was an instinctive country boy. He was happy as long as they were out somewhere with the dogs, looking for birds' nests, or fungi, or badger setts, or creeping up quietly to the meadow in the hope of spotting a deer. He liked playing with the goats, and every week he fed the chickens. The only thing he hated was when the weather drove them indoors to the classroom. He'd rather get soaked to the skin in a field than be bored to tears in front of a whiteboard. Hilary felt she was beginning to understand why he'd failed to thrive at school, but she didn't want to let him off written work altogether.

As with all the other children who were able to do so, she told Simon she would like him to write a diary about his time at Greatwood. At once his little face fell.

'Let's make it a game,' she suggested. 'We'll talk first about what you want to say, then maybe I could write one word and you write the next.'

'OK,' he agreed. 'But if I go first does that mean I get to do all the shortest words and you do the longest ones?'

She laughed at his calculation. They started off that way, writing on the whiteboard and competing with each other to see who got the shortest and who got the longest words. Hilary realised that handwriting was tricky for him. It seemed to take him a long time to remember the shapes of each letter and then get his hand to trace them, so she decided to see how he got on when typing on her personal laptop. This was not something she'd done with any other children, and she didn't plan to make a habit of it, but Simon was able to type so much more quickly than he could write and it seemed to help his confidence.

Still, he soon began to get fidgety when they were stuck in the classroom for long, so Hilary came up with another idea. She suggested they took photographs to go in his diary. Every week they would take a picture of whatever they had been up to, print it off on the office printer, and stick it alongside any words he had written. The key was to keep moving on to the next activity before Simon's attention wandered.

His diary began to look very attractive, and Hilary persuaded him to try handwriting again. She would write one sentence and he would write the next, and they competed to see who could invent the shortest sentences that still made sense.

'At the end of the course, you can take it home to show your mum,' she told him.

'Can I really? That's brilliant!'

'You could take it to school to show your teacher as well.'

His face fell. 'I hate school.'

Hilary asked, 'How does it make you feel when you wake up in the morning and remember you have to go to school that day?'

'Sick,' he said.

'Why do you think that is?'

'I dunno.'

Hilary asked how he thought a new horse would feel when it arrived at Greatwood and was led out to the field to join all the other horses.

'Scared?' he suggested.

'What if the other horses were good at something that he wasn't quite so good at? How would he feel then?'

'Sad?'

Hilary watched his face and could tell he was making the connection. 'But maybe the new horse is good at something that the others aren't good at?'

'Like what?'

'I don't know – maybe it's a really good hurdler and the others can't jump hurdles. Like you, for example. You are really good with your hands. You're good at woodwork and gardening and looking after animals. The other kids in your class might be better than you at writing but I bet none of them could make a nesting box as good as the one you made. I think you'll end up working outdoors one day because you're not an indoors person. You just have to persevere at school for a few more years so that you get some qualifications to help you get a good job. Do you think you can manage that?'

'I suppose.'

'And when you're feeling sick about going to school in the morning, just remember that there are things you are very good at. Think about what you would say to that scared horse going out into the field.'

'OK,' he agreed.

Hilary was sad to see him leave on his last day, clutching his diary. Having nearly said she couldn't take him, he had turned into one of the most rewarding pupils she'd worked with to date. She kept in touch with his social worker and was delighted to hear that he had been found a place in another mainstream school where he was getting extra tuition for his dyslexia. Now all he needs to do is hang on for another six years.

* * *

Simon wasn't the only school phobic who was sent to Greatwood. Shortly after he left, Hilary had another very anxious child referred to her, this one called James. Instead of being disruptive in class, James was withdrawn and depressed. He struggled with dyslexia and got himself into a panic about reading out loud or having to produce any written work. This fear escalated until he panicked if the teacher asked him even the simplest of questions in front of his classmates. His self-esteem was at rock bottom. He wouldn't mix with other children, and he'd just sit at his desk with a worksheet in front of him, frozen with fear and unable to perform. The school sent him to Greatwood in the hope that it might calm him down a little and help build his confidence.

When he stepped out into the yard, everything about James looked timid. His shoulders were hunched up as if he wanted to shrink his head down between them like a turtle. His eyes were darting round on the lookout for danger. Hilary worried that he would be scared of the animals but, on the contrary, he bent down to pet the dogs, and when they went in to meet the horses, he put his hand out to stroke them on the nose quite happily. He took to grooming like a natural and didn't mind getting dirty when asked to clean out the chicken coop or muck out a horse's stable.

When she introduced him to Toyboy, Hilary explained that he was a temperamental pony, very difficult to catch in the paddock, and that he hated loud noises and sudden movements. Something about this seemed to strike a chord with James. He approached Toyboy very carefully, put his hand out slowly and spoke to him in a low, soothing voice that was almost a whisper. Toyboy responded by coming towards him and letting himself be stroked.

'He's sweet,' James told Hilary afterwards. 'I really like him.'

'In that case, he can be your special responsibility while you are here,' she said. 'You can be the one to feed him, groom him and muck out his stable.'

Once he had been shown all that needed to be done, Hilary left them alone with each other, just glancing round the doorway from time to time to check they were OK. Pony and boy would be standing close to each other, almost in a trance as James brushed him down and spoke to him quietly.

'I love it here because it's so peaceful,' he told Hilary with a big sigh.

She mused that she couldn't think of any other ten-year-old boys who sought out peaceful situations. Most of them wanted high-energy computer games and ball sports, and conversations that were conducted at shouting pitch with thumping music in the background. But James wanted peace.

Hilary had done a lot of work with dyslexic children over the years, so she was keen to get James into the classroom and find out where his specific problems lay. He was only young and should still be able to make progress.

What made her very sad was when fifteen-year-olds came to her unable to read or write and just counting the days until they could leave school. Their lives were going to be severely handicapped, but James still had the chance to reach a level of competence that wouldn't hold him back.

'I don't like spelling,' he told her.

'English is a very difficult language to learn,' she replied. 'We've got lots of weird spellings that don't make any sense at all. While you're here, if you need to use a word with a tricky spelling then I will write it on the whiteboard for you and you just need to copy it. How's that for a deal?'

'OK,' he agreed.

At the end of each session, he wrote a diary, as did all the other children who went on the course if they were able to. His was full of misspellings but Hilary didn't correct them. That's not what she was there for. She gave him the correct spelling of a word if he asked for it, but otherwise she just let him write whatever he wanted to say in his own way. It was all perfectly comprehensible, and it was touching the way he kept emphasising the peace and quiet at Greatwood, and his love for Toyboy, the little pony who didn't like loud noises.

'What is the thing you least like about school?' Hilary asked him.

'We're always having tests,' he replied. 'I hate tests. There are so many questions and there's never enough time and it's scary.'

Hilary nodded sympathetically. 'Tests are difficult,' she said. 'I bet you don't want to go to school in the morning on the days you have a test.'

'We have tests all the time. I never want to go to school. I wish I could just come and work here instead.'

'Maybe when you're a bit older,' she smiled. Lots of children who came to Greatwood wanted to know if we had part-time jobs for them. If we'd accepted all the requests to volunteer we would have been over-run in no time.

After a one-to-one course, Hilary usually writes a report for the child's school about positive ways she has found to work with them and what they achieved over their time together. In James's report she wrote about his aptitude with the animals and the progress they'd made in writing, as well as his increased confidence.

I hope James was able to take something of the peace and calm of Greatwood away with him at the end of his ten weeks. He passed our Horse Power programme with flying colours, and looked proud as punch at the awards ceremony. Poor spelling doesn't matter when you're caring for ponies. There are much more important skills in life.

Chapter 19

Dealing with Bullies

Children can be horribly cruel when a herd mentality takes over. They want to fit in and be accepted by their peers, and they think that ganging up on someone who is just a little bit different from them reinforces their own position at the centre of the crowd. The psychology of bullies is complex but the effect on the victim is almost always to drain their self-esteem, leaving them feeling worthless and undeserving. Sometimes scars can be created that stay with the child for life. Many of the children who come to Greatwood have been bullied because of their learning difficulties, or because their behaviour is a little bit different from the norm, and it just compounds the existing problem.

Hermione is one example. She had profound dyslexia and couldn't cope with the curriculum at her mainstream school. By the age of nine, her life was being made a misery by classroom bullies who sniggered every time she got an answer wrong, made faces at her behind the teacher's back and imitated her speech during break time. Even the girls she had considered to be friends sometimes joined in and she was left feeling that she didn't know whom she could trust.

Every day after her mum Tina picked her up from school, she sobbed all the way home in the back seat. Every day there was an incident of some kind and Hermione changed from a sunny little girl to being miserable and withdrawn most of the time.

Tina tried many times to talk to her about it. 'They're the ones who are ignorant, not you,' she explained. 'They don't know what they're talking about. You're a bright girl, brighter than most of them probably, but you have a type of word blindness. It's bad luck but you'll get through it. They, on the other hand, are going to grow up as thoughtless and uncaring individuals if someone doesn't deal with them.'

Hermione couldn't accept this. 'It's my fault,' she said. 'I shouldn't be at that school because I'm not good enough. I should go to a school for dummies.'

'Is that what they said to you?' Tina asked sharply, and Hermione nodded.

It was heartbreaking for a mother to watch her child losing all self-esteem. At weekends, Hermione would go off wandering round the fields on her own, or she would sit indoors playing with the family dogs, and Tina could tell she was getting more and more depressed. She walked slowly, with the weight of the world on her shoulders, watching the clock and dreading going to bed on Sunday night because it meant when she woke up it would be Monday morning and time for another five days of school.

Tina was at her wits' end, when something wonderful happened that would turn the situation on its head. A new headmistress joined the school, heard about the way Hermione was being victimised, and phoned Tina with an idea.

'Hermione tells me that she likes animals and I wondered if she would like to go and visit a place called Greatwood, where she'll be able to work with their rescue horses. I'd be happy to refer her if you agree.'

Tina had heard about Greatwood and she said straight away, 'Yes, please. Definitely. She'd love it.'

The headmistress spoke to Hilary, and it was arranged that Hermione would come for one-to-one sessions on Friday afternoons. It would be her treat at the end of the week, something to look forward to, to help her get through the rest of the days.

Hermione loved Greatwood from the moment she got out of the car that very first afternoon. She was used to being around animals so she wasn't nervous of the dogs or the goats or even the Thoroughbreds. During her second visit, she was allowed to start grooming the animals and her favourite was Poncho, the Shetland with the fluffy black coat. He needed a lot of grooming and Hermione was more than happy to give it.

She was also keen on Marnie, a light bay mare whose foal, Fifi, had sustained a serious injury when she put her leg through a fence, cutting the tendon. Fifi had to be kept in stables while her leg was healing and although she had already been weaned, she needed the company of her mother to keep her calm. Like most mares, Marnie was pretty glad that her nursing days were over and she resented having to be confined to barracks while all her pals were out in the summer sunshine. She was unimpressed by her enforced lack of freedom and used to stomp around the stable, frustrated at being cooped up and dying to get back outside to stretch her legs.

Hilary explained to Hermione the reason for Marnie's frustration, and suggested that maybe she identified with her because she was an outdoors person who hated being stuck indoors herself. She also suggested that she might feel a kinship with Marnie because they had similar names. Whatever the reason, the two soon struck up a relationship. Every Friday when Hermione came to visit, she'd pop in to visit Marnie and Fifi, to see how they were doing. Before she finished her course, Fifi was cured and mother and foal were back outside again.

Each week, Hilary did a little work with Hermione on her reading and writing. She was an intelligent girl with plenty to say, but when she wrote a sentence Hilary was hard-pressed to read it because the letters were shaped so poorly and the spelling was so bad. Hilary knew there were effective ways of dealing with this particular type of dyslexia, and she had a chat with the headmistress at Hermione's school about some strategies that could help.

Hilary talked to Hermione about the bullying as well. 'Has anyone been mean to you this week?' she would ask.

'Well, they all laughed when I got the answer wrong in history today. It was my fault because I meant to say "Armada" but it came out wrong, which was really embarrassing.'

'And do the other children in your class never ever pronounce a word incorrectly themselves? Do they always get the answer right?'

Hermione seemed to think that they did, and Hilary shook her head sceptically. 'I don't believe it.'

By week three, though, a change was occurring. Hermione reported: 'All the other girls were asking me about Greatwood this morning and they were really jealous when they heard I get to help with the horses. They wish they could come as well.'

Hilary smiled. 'This is *your* special time, not theirs. You deserve it.'

Hermione started working towards her Horse Power certificate, learning the names of all the brushes used in the stable, and how to care for the different animals on the farm. Her confidence was visibly growing, and she lit up with pride when Hilary quizzed her about aspects of horse care and she got every single answer right. There was never the slightest doubt that she would be awarded the certificate. If we handed out an award for Keenest Pupil on the Farm, she would have got that one as well.

Her mum came to talk to me at the presentation ceremony. 'You've given me back the old Hermione,' she said. 'She's her smiling, cheerful self again, quite different from the way she was before she came here. I can't thank you enough.'

'It was our pleasure,' I said.

Tina was so grateful for our help that she and a mutual friend Rachel, the wife of Alan King, a top National Hunt trainer, undertook a sponsored walk up the Inca Trail to Macchu Picchu. It's only twenty-six miles but most of that is uphill over rough terrain, and you have to spend at least ten days out there to acclimatise to the high altitude or you risk altitude sickness. She made it, though, and raised a very welcome £3,000 for the Greatwood coffers.

Tina also decided to get a pony for Hermione to keep at home – a little one called Dilly – and that made her the envy of all her classmates. Everyone was clamouring to be her friend so they could come back and meet her pony and even have a ride. Hermione has decided she wants to be a flat racer when she grows up so she'll need all the experience she can get.

Meanwhile, she's started at a new school where her dyslexia is being treated with all the most modern strategies and she has completely put the old, sad days behind her. She doesn't appear to be any the worse now for the difficult times when she was bullied because she couldn't read.

It's much harder, however, to overcome some of the more severe behavioural disorders. Larry has Asperger syndrome, a form of autism in which affected children have well-developed speech and may be very good at schoolwork, particularly maths and IT, but they are not good at social interaction. They find it hard to empathise with others so conversation can be a bit one-sided. Larry tended to get fixated on things like computer games, which he could play for hours without a break. He liked superhero and villain characters in comic books because he could understand them, but the behaviour of other teenagers, flirting and joshing with each other, went right over his head. He didn't understand jokes or teenager-speak. He liked everything to be straightforward and logical and routine.

Larry was attending a mainstream school and his life was made miserable by the jibes of 'geek!' and 'moron!' and worse. Over the years this had made him withdraw even more, back to his computers and comic books. He hated changes to his normal daily routine, but the teachers felt it was important to bring him to Greatwood to see if it could help restore his damaged self-esteem.

Larry came with a group of other children and he hung back on the edge of the crowd, not making eye contact with anyone. In the classroom, he slumped over his desk, not joining in. Hilary thought he looked very lonely and was determined to find some way of helping him, but when they got out to the yard, he was nervous of the animals. He wouldn't come forward to stroke the horses, and he flinched and looked as though he wanted to turn on his heels and run when the dogs came bounding over.

Once again, Hilary decided to use Toyboy, our trusty Shetland pony, because although he's a lively character in many respects, he seems to have a natural affinity with the quiet, withdrawn children who come to the farm. On their first tour round the stables, Hilary told Larry about Toyboy.

'He hates loud noises and sudden movements. They make him very jumpy and he runs away, so it needs someone kind and gentle to look after him.' She could tell Larry was listening, although he didn't respond directly. 'Here he is.' She pointed out Toyboy's unusual brown and white markings. 'Isn't he lovely?'

Larry nodded.

'I don't suppose you could hold him for me? Just for a minute.' Without giving him a chance to say no, she handed over the rope and Larry took it cautiously.

'You can talk to him in a low voice. He likes that. I'll be back in just a minute.'

She guided the rest of the group to the next stable, and when she glanced back, she could see Larry whispering something to Toyboy and stroking his mane. That was a good start.

Suddenly one of the children shrieked as a horse mistook her blonde hair for a handful of straw. The rest of the kids burst out laughing as Hilary extricated her. Then a strident voice rang out: 'Will you please be quiet. You're scaring Toyboy.' It was Larry.

Someone at the back of the crowd hissed, 'Ooh, listen to geek-boy telling us to shut up!'

Hilary strained to see who had spoken, but all the kids were laughing and it could have been one of about three of them. 'Yes, you're quite right, Larry,' she said. 'Could everybody please pipe down?'

She showed the children how to groom the ponies and asked Larry to carry on holding Toyboy steady while two other kids brushed her. 'You're good with him,' she said. 'He's responding well to you. He seems very calm.'

But the minute she turned her back she heard more snide comments being directed towards Larry so she decided to say something to the children back in the classroom at break time.

'We've got some geese on the farm,' she told them, 'and a young goose started bullying the older geese. He would barge up and peck them, or squawk loudly right beside them, and they became scared of him. What do you think we should have done about it?'

The children were interested and all started making suggestions. 'Put the young one in a separate field so it got lonely.' 'Give more treats to the older ones and not the young one.' 'Give it a kick,' one boy suggested, and Hilary had to explain that animal cruelty would not be tolerated on the farm.

'How do you think the older geese, the ones who were being bullied, would feel?' she asked.

'Sad.' 'Upset.' 'Scared.' They looked round at each other.

'Yes, probably all of these things. We had to make a separate bed for the older geese in the chicken shed, so they didn't get picked on at night. That must have made them feel very isolated.'

'Do you have any bullies at your school?' she continued, and there was much shaking of heads.

'No, not really.' 'Can't think of any.'

Hilary persevered. 'No one who gets called names at all?'

There was silence apart from a shuffling of feet.

'That's great,' she said. 'You must be a really nice bunch then.'

Later on, she showed them the chicken shed, and the place where the separate bed for the two older geese had been.

As they walked on, one boy drew up alongside her. 'Why do you think that younger goose was being a bully?' he asked.

'I don't know. Why do *you* think?'

'Perhaps he was scared of something himself.'

'Yes,' Hilary agreed. 'That's possible.' In fact, she wasn't sure that geese have a particularly wide repertoire of emotions, but it was interesting to get the children speculating.

After that, she didn't overhear anyone calling Larry names any more so the message seemed to have sunk in to an extent – or maybe they were just waiting until she was out of earshot.

Hilary spent some time with Larry and while conversation could be difficult, because he didn't understand the normal to and fro rhythm and would frequently interrupt her with non sequiturs, she grew very fond of him. He was clever and insightful about the animals, and she pointed that out to him. Gradually she could see his confidence growing. He was still nervous around the bigger horses but he considered himself the expert on Toyboy, the only one who knew how to keep him calm.

'Don't worry, Toyboy, I'm looking after you,' Hilary heard him whisper one day and he continued to speak out if anyone was being noisy or boisterous in their vicinity. What was interesting was that he was empathising with the pony's feelings – and empathy is notoriously difficult for those with Asperger syndrome. They generally find it very hard to put themselves in another person's shoes.

Larry earned his certificate and seemed to have gained confidence as a result of his time at Greatwood. I just hope it lasted when he got back to school. In classrooms, as in herds of horses, you get some dominant characters who want to be herd leader, and others who are naturally more submissive. I tend to take this into account when I decide who to stable each horse with, and which field to turn them out into. For example, it was clear from the start that Deano's Beano wanted to be 'top dog' and would never back down in conflict, so I tried to avoid putting him in a situation where it might arise. But you haven't got the luxury of arranging children in a school into different classrooms according to their temperaments.

Towards the end of Larry's time at the farm, Hilary was walking with one of the teachers back towards the minibus and they passed the geese pecking by the side of the lane.

'I was meaning to ask you,' the teacher said. 'What did you do about that stroppy goose that was bullying the others? Did you ever come up with a solution?'

'Yes,' Hilary said, with a deadpan expression. 'But I'm not sure our solution would work for your children. We ate it!'

Chapter 20

Paul and Just Jim

Just Jim was a leggy bay horse who'd had a successful National Hunt career with a number of wins. Usually National Hunt horses are easier to rehome than flat racers because they are trained over a longer period and are used to being turned out in the field, but I'd been told that Jim had had a nasty accident in one race when another horse crashed into him at speed, causing him to topple over, and he ended up at the bottom of a multi-horse pile-up. He suffered a number of health problems after that and it gradually became clear that his racing career was over. His owners thought the world of him and wanted us to make sure he had a safe and secure future.

Just Jim had come to us round about the same time as Tim. We always find that partnering new horses together settles them much better before we turn them out into the herd. They seemed fine in the stable together, just regarding each other with mild interest, although it was frustrating to find that Jim was another crib-biter.

It was with some trepidation that we put them out into the field together for the first time because as far as we knew, Tim hadn't been turned out before. He was the one we were keeping a close eye on, but he just took it in his stride and immediately lowered his head to graze. Jim, on the other hand, hurtled about at full tilt and ricocheted off fences and gates. Tim lifted his head with mild interest to watch Jim running amok. We had expected Tim to be over-excited but not Jim, which just goes to show you can't take anything for granted. Jim clearly needed a little more time to settle and get to know us, and he was probably missing his old friends and surroundings. It took a while for him to calm down, but eventually Tim's quiet, sober influence took effect, and the two of them became good pals, often seen grazing nostril to nostril.

We had hoped that we could rehome Jim as his previous owners had wished but investigations on his back showed that he wasn't up to being ridden anymore, so we decided to use him in the Horse Power programme. He was a steady horse when he wanted to be, usually even-tempered and gentle enough to let children fuss over him. There were just a few mornings when he woke up on the wrong side of the stable and wouldn't cooperate. He would be fidgety and grumpy, standing at the back with his ears flattened to his head, and no amount of coaxing would change his mood. What caused it? A disturbed night? Gas pains from his crib-biting? Who knows? We learned that on days when he had a strop on, it was easier just to leave him and work with other horses instead.

Just Jim did his job but he didn't form a special relationship with any particular child, until he met a tiny fourteen-year-old mildly autistic boy with floppy white blond hair, whose name was Paul.

Paul was a serious child, who was perfectly bright and articulate but who didn't seem to be engaged by anything. He wandered round in his own little world, quite separate from the other children in his group. He listened to the instructions he was given and followed them to the letter, and he always gave the correct answer to any questions Hilary asked, but he didn't seem to be affected by the animals or anything that was going on around him.

On the first tour to meet the animals, we usually get a range of reactions from the children: there are those who are nervous, those who want to rush up and cuddle and stroke the animals straight away, and others who are awestruck. The goats always get a big reaction with their barging and pushing and the strident 'behhh' sound they make as they clamour for attention and – by extension – food treats. Paul walked round watching the animals with the rest of them, but there was no emotional reaction. Occasionally he stretched out a hand to touch a horse's nose but it was as though he only did it because the others were, not because he wanted to do so himself.

Hilary picked up different pieces of equipment that they had discussed in the classroom and asked about each, 'Who can tell me what this is called?' Every time she asked Paul, she'd get the right answer – 'curry comb,' 'hoof pick' – but he'd be unsmiling and his eyes never met hers. The shock of white hair often fell across his face and he'd flick it back, gazing just over the shoulder of whomever was speaking to him.

When they went into the classroom for break time, Paul remained detached and didn't join in any of the conversations. He ate and drank noisily, slurping his juice, chomping on biscuits and belching loudly.

'We don't do that here, Paul,' Hilary told him. 'Try to eat quietly so no one else can hear you.'

'He's copying the animals' eating habits so they don't feel embarrassed,' one of the children joked, but Paul didn't respond. Autistic children can struggle to understand humour. They like straightforward statements of fact, and find it difficult to pick up nuances.

It was hard to communicate with Paul because of his lack of reaction to everything. It's a common pattern with autism and it can be difficult to be around, because you don't feel as though you're getting through, but Hilary was determined to persevere. Never say never.

It was during Paul's second visit to Greatwood that she took the children to the stable that Tim and Jim shared. Tim came forward eagerly to meet the visitors but Jim was having one of his grumpy days and stood at the back of the stable with his ears flattened to his head.

'He's not in the mood for company today,' Hilary explained. 'Some days he is and other days he's not.' She was explaining how you can read a horse's mood from the position of its ears, when Paul suddenly pushed to the front and stood on tiptoe to see over the partition into Jim's stall. He wanted a proper look at this horse.

Noticing the shock of blond hair, Jim did something quite extraordinary for him: he wandered over to investigate. Usually when he was in a bad mood, Jim couldn't be roused by anything except his lunch, so this was noteworthy, but what followed was even more astonishing. He craned his neck downwards so that it was touching Paul's hand where it rested on top of the partition. Paul reached up and tickled his nose. For several minutes Jim stood still in a quite uncomfortable position that enabled Paul to reach his face and when he lifted his head away, Hilary could see Paul's face flushed with excitement.

'I've never seen him do that before,' she commented. 'Lucky you! Perhaps you would like to groom Jim?'

'OK,' Paul said, nodding emphatically.

Hilary gave him the brushes and was impressed to see that he remembered exactly what to do with them from the demonstration she'd given earlier. So he *did* listen to her! Jim stood and let him work, only occasionally shifting position when he had been still too long, and behaving in an uncharacteristically cooperative way. There was an expression on Paul's face that Hilary hadn't seen before, a spark of interest in his eyes. He was enjoying himself.

From that moment on, grooming Jim became the highlight of Paul's visits to Greatwood. Whether Jim was in his stable or out in the field, he would come over as soon as he saw Paul, and he always let Paul groom him, although he would frequently refuse to let others get close. This was a source of great pride to Paul. He'd been allocated the 'difficult' horse to look after, and it would only behave for him, not for anyone else.

Paul became fanatical about keeping Jim spick and span. 'Someone's put the brushes back all dirty,' he would complain. 'I can't use these or I'll make his coat dirty.'

Every week he made a fuss because the brushes weren't cleaned to his high standards and he would ostentatiously clean them before starting work on Jim's coat. The staff laughingly told him he was just like Aggie MacKenzie, one of the women on the television programme *How Clean Is Your House?*, but to Paul cleanliness was a serious business.

It was gratifying that he was able to form such a close relationship with Jim, but Hilary wanted to work on some other aspects of his behaviour as well. She tried to explain to him about jokes, that sometimes people say things for a laugh rather than because they really mean it. He frowned at this.

'But why? Why would they say it if it's not true?'

Hilary tried her best, but how do you explain what a sense of humour is? He must have understood to an extent, though, because later that day when she was sitting having a cup of tea with the teachers, Paul came up to them.

'I'm working harder than you are,' he said. 'The horses look forward to me coming because I do them properly and no one else does.'

Hilary was taken aback until his face spread into a wide grin. 'That's a joke!' he told her. 'Don't you get it?'

From then on, it became a subject of much yard banter that Paul was the one who did all the work at Greatwood and the rest of us just lazed around. He thought it was hilarious, and we all laughed too, delighted that he had discovered a sense of humour.

Hilary got through to him in a few other ways, such as getting him to improve his eating and drinking habits. She found out that he lived alone with his dad, who obviously hadn't been prioritising table manners, but once his sloppy, noisy habits were pointed out he tried his best to change them. You only ever had to tell him something once. In fact, he used to astonish Hilary by quoting verbatim little throwaway comments she had made several weeks earlier.

'You told us they used to have a goat at Greatwood who thought it was a dog.'

'You told us that a hen called Flirty Gertie used to stow away in the back of the car and jump out when it got to the shops.'

'You said that it costs £100 a week to keep a horse.'

Half the time Hilary couldn't remember saying these things, and if she had, it hadn't seemed as though Paul was taking them in, but in fact he remembered absolutely everything he was told.

Hilary could tell that he was enjoying himself but she was still touched when one of the teaching assistants who accompanied Paul's group told her that he used to count the days between each visit. 'As it gets close, he'll be jumping up and down with excitement. "Three days to Greatwood, two days to Greatwood, Greatwood tomorrow ..."' In the car on the way there, she said he'd literally be shaking with excitement.

Paul passed the tests with flying colours and was one of a group of fifteen students who was to receive a certificate. Once again, National Hunt jockey Mick Fitzgerald kindly agreed to present the awards and when he came into the classroom the children were speechless with excitement. He spoke to them about his background, told them that if they liked horses they should make sure they pursued that interest and didn't let anything stand in their way, then he commended them on gaining the qualification.

After the presentations, they all went out to the yard and Just Jim was in one of his grumpy moods, making faces at any passersby, including Mick. But then he saw Paul and that was different. Paul hurried over and gave Jim a cuddle, and Jim bent his head down to nuzzle against him. Hilary took some photographs and sent Paul copies afterwards. She had the impression that he wasn't normally a demonstrative boy, and these pictures highlighted the huge change in him.

He'd come a long way from the little schoolboy who had wandered round Greatwood during his first visit, listening but not showing any interest. He'd found someone to care about. Just for a while, he'd broken out of the self-contained world of autism and learned how to engage, not just with animals but with his fellow human beings as well.

Chapter 21

Further along the Autism Spectrum ...

There are so many shades and degrees of autism that a great number of experts argue they shouldn't all be lumped together as one disorder. Paul, whom we discussed in the last chapter, has high-functioning autism, with a greater than average IQ, and one day he is likely to be able to hold down a job, particularly in an area such as IT where his poorer than average communication skills will not necessarily hold him back. He might well get married, have children and lead a fairly normal life, because although he doesn't instinctively understand social interaction, he has been able to learn certain skills by observing and listening to those around him.

At Greatwood, we also get visits from children right at the other end of the autism spectrum, who have such severe problems to contend with that they will never live independent lives. They may be mute, with significant cognitive problems, and prone to repetitive behaviour, such as rocking and flapping their hands. Such children can get anxious very easily, especially if they are thrust into new environments amongst unfamiliar faces, and part of our job is to lower their anxiety levels and help them feel secure.

Autism is far more common in boys than in girls, but we had one visitor to Greatwood who was a very pretty little nine-year-old girl called Daisy. She had long, dark hair and an exquisite face with almond-shaped brown eyes. But she was mute, and she rocked back and forwards a lot, and she was petrified of what she might find on the farm. As her teacher led her off the minibus, she tried to shrink back and hide, eyes darting from side to side in case of danger.

There were six children in that group. Hilary led them straight into the classroom, where she had laid out lots of the little pictures that form part of what is known as the Picture Exchange Communication System, or PECS (similar to the system that had been used by the mute group Elizabeth took round a couple of years earlier). The children were being taught to communicate by putting together the appropriate picture cards. For example, if they wanted a drink, they had to pick the card that said 'I WANT' and stick it on a strip of Velcro together with a picture of a drink, and give it to one of their carers. Each child had a little dictionary of pictures to choose from, but it could still be very frustrating for them when they couldn't communicate precisely what they wanted to say, or couldn't find the exact card they needed at the moment they wanted it. Frustration was expressed through tantrums, shrieking or throwing things to the floor. This was a regular occurrence, which the staff who had accompanied them would rush to deal with.

When working with children like these, it was important that everything was explained to them in a clear and straightforward way, with no sudden surprises. There shouldn't be lots of new faces for them to get used to because even one is a struggle.

To help the children understand what they were going to be doing at Greatwood, Hilary had written the time-table for the morning on her whiteboard – 10am walk around the farm; 10.30am meet the goats; 10.45am meet the horses; 11.15am snack break in the classroom – and beside each item there was a corresponding picture. She talked through the plan, explaining each part of it and what they would be able to do when they got there, and then they all set off.

Little Daisy managed the walk around the farm, but she shrank back if any animals came close. Hilary noticed she seemed particularly scared of the chickens, and she could identify with that because as a young girl she used to be scared of them herself. Her mother kept chickens and would make her crawl into the chicken coop to collect the fresh eggs, and Hilary used to be terrified of their flapping. She eventually got over her fear but can still remember it all too clearly, so when Daisy shrank back from the chickens she felt very sympathetic.

When they reached the goat shed, Hilary had some slices of bread for the children to feed to them. She demonstrated first.

'You post the bread into their mouth the way you would post a letter into a letterbox. Don't worry. They won't bite you.'

Some brave souls took their pieces of bread and giggled as they disappeared into the goats' mouths so quickly it was like a magic trick: now you see it, now you don't.

After they had finished with the goats, it was time to go over to the stables to meet some of the horses. The group turned and Hilary just happened to be standing next to Daisy. As she stepped out across the yard towards the stable, Daisy panicked, reached up and grabbed a handful of Hilary's hair. Hilary tried to disentangle her fingers but the grip was too tight and she was pulling really hard. Two of the teachers rushed over to intervene.

'Daisy, let go! It's OK, you're safe. You can let go!'

Daisy was in panic mode and her fingers had locked into position. Hilary's scalp was aching when the teacher finally prised Daisy away, and she rubbed at it ruefully.

'Daisy, you don't have to come into the stables if you don't want,' she said, 'but why don't you stand just at the door here so you can see what is going on? One of your teachers will stand with you.'

So Daisy stood and rocked in the doorway, caught up in her own little world, as the others went in to meet a few of the horses.

It wasn't just fear of the animals that Daisy had to contend with. Like a lot of children with autism, she was hypersensitive to smell and sound. Certain areas at Greatwood are pretty smelly, and the horses can make quite a high-pitched sound as they call to each other. We kept the dogs indoors during this particular group's visiting times and instructed Edward not to use the Billy Goat, which can get noisy, but still you could see the children jump at the slightest sound. If someone dropped a saddle and the buckles clattered on the concrete floor, if a car pulled into the yard and scared the chickens, making them screech, or if a child yelled in panic as a horse shifted position, it could set the whole group on edge, and Daisy seemed more sensitive than most.

To her, the world was a huge place full of random, unconnected people, animals, events, sounds and stimuli, and she couldn't put them together in her head to understand cause and effect, action and reaction. She couldn't predict the consequences of any event, so she always feared the worst. It was a horribly anxious way to live.

The basic Horse Power course can be adapted to suit the abilities and needs of the different groups that visit. Sometimes the focus is on raising self-esteem and building confidence, sometimes it's on working as part of a team and cooperation, but with children like Daisy, it's beneficial for them simply to be exposed to a new environment with new stimuli and to learn to deal with it. It had to be fun as well, so every week there was a game to play. In the first week, they played a game with the grooming kit and some coloured buckets.

'Who can put the dandy brush in the pink bucket?' Hilary asked, and when someone had managed that, it would be, 'Can someone put the curry comb in the blue bucket?' Most of the children joined in, but not Daisy.

'I don't think I'm going to get anywhere with her,' Hilary mused to me after the visit. 'I don't think she is going to engage. You win some, you lose some.'

The following week, when that particular group arrived, Hilary set up a game involving the animals' food. Each child had some pictures of types of food on Velcro sheets, and they talked about which animals like which kinds of food, then they went out on a kind of puzzle trail round the farm. As they reached each stable or field, they came across a sign with the animal's name: 'My name's Steady Eddy and I like …' They had to remember that Steady Eddy liked carrots, take a picture of a carrot from their Velcro strip and stick it on the sign.

Some of the children could remember feeding bread to the goats the previous week, so when they got to the goats' stall, they stuck the bread picture beside it. Likewise, there was a bag of grain to go beside the chickens. And Hilary had explained to them that Potentate, like many horses, likes extra-strong mints, so there was a picture of a packet of mints to stick on the sign next to Po's field.

Daisy was trembling with fear when they got up to the field where the horses were running around. She shrunk back behind the others, but she still managed to stick on the correct food pictures, so it proved she was listening at least.

When they got to the area where the hens were wandering around, Hilary made sure Daisy was standing well out of the way before letting the braver children throw them a handful of chicken feed. Immediately they came right up, squawking and pecking the ground at the children's feet. Daisy was shaking and clinging to her teacher's arm but she kept watching from a safe distance rather than trying to run away. She was scared but at the same time she didn't want to miss anything.

Back at the stables, Daisy once again stood by the entrance, rocking back and forwards, but something very interesting happened while the others were inside. Robbie appeared from round the corner leading Tim towards his stable. Before the teacher had time to hurry Daisy out of the way, they were already passing. Suddenly Daisy's little hand shot out and she touched Tim on the rump, just quickly. It seemed she wanted to know what his coat felt like. The teacher didn't comment but she mentioned it to Hilary later and they decided that it was a hopeful sign. Each week, they agreed, they would bring Daisy a little closer to the horses to see whether she tried touching them again.

During the third visit, Daisy was still getting used to the environment and standing well back from the animals, but on week four, when the other children were brushing the goats, Hilary glanced round and saw her straining in their direction as if she wanted to join in but was too scared at the same time. Without making a big deal of it, Hilary handed her a brush and stood back to give her room to draw closer if she wanted to.

Daisy thought about it for a long time. Most of the group had finished and handed back their brushes when Daisy suddenly made a decision. She stepped forward, extended her arm as far as it would go, and ran her brush over the back of one of the goats. Her body language was a contradictory mixture: she wanted to brush that goat while keeping as far away from it as she possibly could. But she did it, and that was the main thing.

Once again, Hilary and the teachers didn't draw attention to her action. They continued as if nothing had happened, and when they got to the stable they led Daisy just a few feet closer to the horses than she had been the previous week.

During week five Hilary put a brush in Daisy's hand while they were in the stables, and she was finally able to reach out and brush the back of a horse. One of the teachers winked at Hilary. Slowly but surely, it was working!

The progress continued over the next few weeks. By week eight, Daisy was able to walk into the goats' enclosure on her own and while she would shriek madly if they turned and came towards her, it was reaction-seeking shrieking rather than the pure terror it had been before. She knew she was safe with them. She could also stroke horses on the neck and back, although she wasn't ever confident enough to touch their noses.

During week eight, Hilary decided it was time to introduce the children to the dogs. In many ways they were scarier than the other animals on the farm because although smaller, they were more boisterous and liable to jump up. They wouldn't bite but they might well lick if you had any exposed skin that they could reach.

It was important for the children to get used to dogs, as they were likely to meet them in their everyday life, just walking along a road, and they'd be at a huge disadvantage if they panicked every time. The school's primary aim in sending this group of children to Greatwood had been to try to drag them out of their cocoons for a short while and help them not to have such incredibly high levels of anxiety around animals. This was going to be the most important test of all.

There was a lot of shrieking as Mabel and Bessie came bounding out, but it was shrieking for effect rather than shrieking provoked by terror, and all the children, including Daisy, were able to bend down and pet them. It may sound like a small achievement when compared with the other children who were passing their certificates, but it was easily of equal magnitude in terms of its significance to their lives.

Chapter 22

Different Kinds of Challenges

Over the years, we've had some groups of children at Greatwood who have huge challenges to confront in their lives. Of these, I always find watching children with cerebral palsy particularly moving, because they struggle so hard to do things the rest of us take for granted. We haven't had any wheelchair-bound children yet – although we're open to it – but cerebral palsy can make walking very difficult.

Children with cerebral palsy have spasms and walk with a strange kind of motion, almost like a puppet, as they struggle to control their muscle coordination. These children are perfectly intelligent, but have difficulty speaking and being understood, and they may have contorted facial movements. It's easy to underestimate their IQ, but in fact cognitive impairment isn't part of the disorder. Imagine being trapped inside a body that won't do what you want it to do, and being fully aware of what you are missing? To me, that would be a nightmare.

Hilary has to adapt the normal curriculum for children with cerebral palsy because they can't manage the long walks around the farm. There is likely to be slightly more classroom activity than normal, but meeting and interacting with the animals is still a major part of the programme. They all undergo physical therapy aimed at helping them to control their movements to an extent, and our goal for them is to learn to stroke the animals with sufficient pressure so that it is enjoyable, but without pressing too hard and hurting them. When they get a positive reaction from the animal in question, they are usually delighted.

I remember watching one little boy called David. He was very unsteady on his feet and leaning against a partition in the stables so as not to lose his balance, while reaching out with his other hand to pet Toyboy's brown and white coat. He was concentrating hard, and the look on his face appeared like a grimace but his carer told me that was him smiling. When it was time to go back to the classroom, he didn't want to leave and no one had the heart to drag him away, so the carer stayed with him. David stroked Toyboy for over an hour that morning, his hand moving gently but firmly. Toyboy had his eyes closed and was in seventh heaven!

We haven't had any visually impaired children yet, although we'd be happy to, as I'm sure they could get a lot out of the Horse Power programme. Most of the hearing-impaired children who come to us either have a hearing aid or they have learned to lip-read. We had one boy in particular, called Adam, who was a complete fidget in the classroom but as soon as his group got outside he tried to take charge of all the others, bossing them around in a booming voice.

'You go and clean out that bucket!' 'Get me the brushes!' 'It's your job to muck out that stall.'

He'd turn away so he wouldn't be able to see them answering back – you know for sure when you've lost the attention of someone who lip-reads, because they aren't looking at you – and it made him quite successful as a dictator. Hilary had to keep an eye on him to make sure he actually did some of the work himself as well as acting as the group manager.

An important part of the Horse Power course concerns teamwork and collaborating with each other. It's a crucial lesson for children, who can tend to be shut off in their own little worlds. Everyone has to pull their weight when working with animals, rather than trying to pass all the trickiest jobs on to someone else. Hilary will never resort to telling someone off, but she will try to find a way of making them realise for themselves that their behaviour has an impact on those around them, and that it's up to them what kind of impact that is.

When a group of girls came to complain to Hilary that Adam wasn't pulling his weight in the mucking-out task they had been given, she decided to show him what it was like to be in a team where the burden wasn't shared equally. She'd noticed that another little boy called Roger didn't seem to have much energy and worked very slowly, so she asked Adam to go and clean out the hen house with him. 'You've got half an hour to finish it,' she told them. 'It needs to be spotless so that the hens don't get sick.'

At the end of the allocated time, Adam approached Hilary. 'It's not fair. Roger hardly did any of the work and I had to do it all.'

Hilary smiled. 'How does it feel when you have to do all the work?'

'It makes me cross.'

'Well, don't you think that's how the girls felt when you got them to do the mucking out while you stood and gave orders?'

She could see a moment of realisation dawning on him. There wasn't going to be a get-out clause for him just because he couldn't hear. At Greatwood, everyone is treated the same, as far as possible.

Physical disadvantages can be more straightforward to deal with than complex learning difficulties, because the child's limitations are more immediately obvious. Hilary had one group of girls aged fourteen and fifteen who had global development delay, a syndrome with many different possible causes in which children are significantly behind their peers in terms of reaching developmental milestones. Some of the girls had the small eyes and smooth upper lips characteristic of foetal alcohol syndrome. The others had normal facial features, but all were very slow to follow what Hilary was saying. Despite their age, they couldn't read or do basic sums, and instructions had to be given in the straightforward way you would speak to a toddler, for example 'open the window' or 'pick up that pen'. If you said to them, 'Please could you go across and open the window, and while you are there pick up the pen that has fallen to the floor,' they would be completely flummoxed. They could only process one piece of information at a time.

Hilary had been told the girls had poor literacy but not that they had problems in all areas of learning, and she had to think on her feet and adjust the plan for the morning to suit them, choosing simple words and short sentences. She was taken aback when she asked one girl a question – 'What kind of thing do you think horses might be scared of?' – and she received the answer, 'Sorry, but I don't actually know.' She wouldn't even hazard a guess for fear of getting it wrong. It was then she realised that, as with so many other groups that visited Greatwood, these girls needed their confidence built up.

Out in the yard, she gave each girl a straightforward task and explained clearly what was to be done. Some were asked to sweep, some to clean brushes, some to wash out feed bowls and water troughs. They worked slowly but were painstaking and she was careful to praise each of them individually.

In the classroom, she knew that it was worth waiting an unusual length of time for the answer and perhaps giving them some clues rather than moving on to ask someone else. With these girls, she found that if she waited in silence for a minute or so, then the answer might eventually come. It was just slower than you'd expect with other children. She started going over the same questions every week. They could remember the answers from last time, which meant they were faster in responding, and they would be inordinately pleased with themselves.

When it came to working with the animals, their slow processing speed was almost an advantage because there were no sudden movements, and grooming sessions were nice and long. Sometimes Hilary looked at her watch, despairing that they would ever finish on time, but rather than rush them onwards, as people probably tended to do in the outside world, she let them work at their own pace. The result was that each week they got better at remembering the order in which to do tasks and where the tools were kept, and they needed less direct help. They took pride in their work. There was one girl who cleaned the hen house so thoroughly you could have eaten your dinner off the floor. She was bright red in the face with the effort, but glowing with delight at the praise she received.

As well as children with learning difficulties, we some-times had visits from gifted and talented children, all of whom had exceptional skills in one or more areas. Some were advanced in maths and science, others in the arts or languages, and a few in virtually everything academic. It can be quite tricky for teachers to keep such children engaged in the learning process, especially in a main-stream school where they have to cater for the majority and time is limited. At Greatwood, Hilary decided to get them thinking about the ethics of the decision-making processes behind the running of the charity. She gave them a PowerPoint presentation about the work we do and then asked questions to spark a debate about how they thought the charity should be run. Should we priori-tise elderly or sick horses that are unlikely to find another home? When a racehorse owned by a syndicate sustains an injury, who has responsibility for its rehabilitation? Who should pay for the care of retired racehorses? The debate became so animated at times that Hilary could scarcely get a word in edgeways.

We sometimes wished we took 'before' and 'after' videos of children coming to Greatwood just to highlight the differences it could make. Probably the most obvious changes occurred with the severely autistic, non-verbal children who arrived in a state of great distress, very anxious about what they would find, but by the time they left after ten weeks, they were happily interacting with the animals and signing 'Goodbye. Thank you' or pulling out picture cards with smiley faces to show us. Children with all kinds of emotional and behavioural difficulties have overcome phobias here or learned to interact with others, and we see a real change in their posture and facial expressions from week one to week ten. Kids who had been too timid to say 'boo!' to a goose became able to stick up for themselves, while bossy, dominant ones calmed down and made some friends.

We knew we were making a difference just by watching, although it was always nice when we got a call from a teacher or parent to tell us that the positive effects had filtered through into their school and home life as well. The children benefited, their families, carers and school benefited, and the horses enjoyed it too. You would be hard-pressed to find any other establishment keeping upwards of fifty horses where they are all quite so impeccably groomed as ours, and we would never manage it without our teams of helpers.

Chapter 23

Greatwood Expands

Hilary is a keen gardener, and by coincidence Michael and I had long been thinking that we would like to introduce a new programme to teach children about wildflowers and plants, because we had such a rich abundance of specimens around Greatwood. Over the years, we have added more acres to the original 42. Every time an adjacent plot of land came up we negotiated with the farmer, took it on and reseeded it so that by the time Hilary came to us we had 230 acres altogether. There was a bluebell wood winding around the fields, a secluded wildflower meadow way up on a hillside where you could spot the occasional deer, and down near the bottom of the farm there was an area with a few apple trees and a profusion of brambles and nettles.

When Hilary took children on walks round the farm, she would often point out the different species of plants then quiz them to see how well they remembered the names. They seemed to like this, and were full of questions of their own, so she agreed with us that a sister programme dealing with horticulture would complement the Horse Power programme nicely.

We cleared the area at the bottom of the farm and planted more apple trees, then dug a small pond where the children could go pond dipping to learn about all the creatures that were living in there. We added a wooden shed that could be used as an outdoor classroom, and a poly tunnel in which to propagate seeds. Hilary had the brilliant idea of allocating to each child their own small patch in which they could plant whatever they liked. We filled some old car tyres with soil, and each one made a perfect space in which a child could create their own miniature garden.

Once Hilary had developed a structure for the gardening course she applied for accreditation. We were delighted when it came through and we could award certificates for a course called 'Developing Skills in Horticulture'. Children who had successfully finished the 'Developing Confidence Through Working with Animals' course could elect to come back and do this as well, and as soon as we announced it the applications began flooding in.

To pass the course, each child was given the responsibility of looking after their own raised bed in a tyre. They were offered a choice of seeds or seedlings and they had to make their own decisions about what to sow and where to plant them. They could have flowers or vegetables or both, and it was their duty to tend their own plots, keeping them neat, well watered and weed-free over the next ten weeks. When we knew a group was coming, we might pre-plant a few things, just to be sure they would be able to see some of the fruits of their labour before they left.

We had thought of most hazards on the farm and fenced off any dangerous areas but the one thing we hadn't reckoned on was rabbits. The children were surprisingly philosophical when they arrived to find their carefully tended courgettes had been munched to the stalk and that the rabbits had even uprooted all the onions. These things happen in the countryside.

What was even more surprising to us was the number of children who refused to eat the vegetables they had grown. The French beans were especially good in the first year the scheme was running and Hilary urged one group of fifteen-year-olds to try eating them raw.

'Ew, no, yuck!' 'It looks disgusting.' 'I don't eat green things.'

She couldn't believe it was possible to reach your mid teens without having tried a green bean but it seemed that was the case, and nothing she could do would persuade them to change their minds.

After those early teething troubles we surrounded the garden area with a rabbit-proof fence so that the children, rather than the rabbits, could enjoy the results of their hard work. And Greatwood had a new course to offer, meaning that Hilary was twice as busy as before and we had to take on a teaching assistant to support her.

As well as gardening and pond dipping, they expanded the activities to teach some survival skills, such as building a den in the outdoors and tracking animals. The children learned to identify different paw prints, and also to spot some of the birds that colonise the area, including peregrine falcons, redwings and jays.

By this stage there were three hundred children a year coming to Greatwood, but the programme was so successful, and the results for the children were so striking, that Michael and I kept talking about ways we could expand our limited facilities. But we were still short of space for taking on additional groups of children. Even if we'd had unlimited funding, there were geographical boundaries beyond which the farm simply couldn't expand without having major roads running through the middle, and there were obvious limits to the strain we could put on our dedicated, long-suffering staff.

Ever the ideas man, Michael came up with a new plan to introduce the Horse Power programme at some of the country's independent schools that had equine facilities. There was much discussion in the media at the time about whether it was right that independent schools should have charitable status, and he reckoned it would help those schools to justify their position if they could offer a course to children in the local community who had special needs. He had a chat with the bursar at Marlborough College, who put him in touch with the Independent Schools' Bursars Association, and through them he was introduced to Danny Anholt, the Director of Riding at Millfield School in Somerset.

Millfield is an iconic school, taking children from all over the world. They place a strong emphasis on sports and keep around a hundred horses in their stables, so it was an ideal place to introduce Horse Power. Danny came to visit Greatwood and was enthusiastic about what we were doing here – so much so that he decided to introduce our programme to Millfield forthwith. Hilary went over to give advice and help get them started. Danny gets Millfield students helping on the course, so it benefits everyone and has been very popular.

Michael and I were delighted to spread the word and in 2008 Bryanston School also adopted Horse Power, following Millfield's lead. Alice Plunkett, the Channel 4 racing commentator, came along to present certificates to the first group to pass the course. We don't charge for passing on the details of our programme, but we hope that the schools in question will perhaps have an open day or do some other kind of fundraising venture to help us at some point.

As well as spreading the word to other institutions, we needed to think about upgrading the facilities at Greatwood. In 2008 we were lucky enough to get a grant from Wooden Spoon, a trust set up by the English Rugby

Union to help physically, mentally or socially disadvan-
taged children, and we used it to convert a stable that
backed onto the classroom into a proper cloakroom. Up
until then, the children had to balance on one leg in the
corridor to put on or take off their boots and outdoor
clothes, or queue up to use the toilet and wash basin –
which wasn't ideal, as many of them were not particularly
patient. We realised that poor Hilary had been preparing
snacks for break-time then washing up all the plates and
cups in a washing-up bowl that she filled from an outdoor
tap, and were amazed she had never complained about it
before.

The new cloakroom meant that there was room in
which to get changed, hooks that the children could hang
their outdoor jackets on, and a bench on which they could
sit down while they wrestled their boots on and off. It also
meant there wouldn't be any more waiting around, so
when they were ready to meet the horses, they could go
straight outside – which was important for children who
were apprehensive about doing so. There was now a
proper kitchen area for making snacks and washing-up,
and a new entrance that meant the children shouldn't be
trapped indoors any longer by a quad bike pushing muck
to the slurry lagoon. We were extremely grateful to the
rugby crowd for this new facility, which we called, rather
grandly, 'The Wooden Spoon Unsaddling Enclosure'.

We contacted Richard Erven, regional chairman of
Wooden Spoon, to ask if he would consider officially

opening the facility for us. I was pretty sure he would be far too busy to come along, so I was staggered when I got the reply that he wouldn't open it himself but that Princess Anne, the Princess Royal, and Wooden Spoon's patron, had agreed to do it. We'd never had a royal visit at Greatwood before and had no idea what it might entail – but I was about to learn.

Some aides turned up first to discuss the plans for the day. We had to have a contingency plan for every eventuality, and that included the ever-present chance of bucketing rain. Jeremy Sumbler, a long-time supporter of Greatwood who provided us with a marquee for our open days each year, agreed to come up with a scheme for covering the yard so that in inclement weather the Princess Royal would be able to walk from barn to barn without getting soaked. We had meetings to decide exactly how long she would spend in each barn, which horses she would meet, the people to whom she would be introduced, and I was fully briefed on my responsibilities in acting as her official guide.

Luckily, many of the horses were still out to grass so the stables wouldn't be full of animals that might get fractious or alarmed by the unaccustomed noise levels, but everything had to be mucked out and scrupulously cleaned so that there wasn't so much as a piece of straw out of place. Some black-covered flooring was put down in the yard, but we found belatedly that it showed every single mark, and poor Sue spent hours on her hands and knees cleaning it in the hours before the Princess Royal arrived.

It seemed only natural to tie in the visit with the presentation of certificates to children who had recently completed the Horse Power programme. Former champion jockey Willie Carson agreed to present them, but it meant that we also needed seating for twenty-two children, along with their parents and carers, and on top of that we had invited some local dignitaries, as well as our most loyal supporters.

The visit was to take place in the early afternoon, so we asked our friend Sally, who was the local caterer, to supply canapés and champagne for our guests, and sandwiches for the children. She took over our office and had a portable oven going on every desk, with trays of food balanced on chairs, shelves and filing cabinets. Needless to say, the dogs had to be kept in our cottage and well out of the way. There was far too much scope for them to mess up our meticulous planning.

Coudy and Lucie, a lovely couple from the Czech Republic, had trained one of our horses, Transpique, in a range of new and special skills. He had learned to kneel, sit on his haunches and lie down when requested, as part of a routine they had prepared for our last open day. Much to our amusement, Transpique could often be seen kneeling in the field to retrieve a tasty morsel from underneath a fence. At times like that, he seemed more like a goat than a gelding. We were confident that he would kneel down impeccably for the Princess Royal. In fact, as he was being led up to the area where he would perform, the trainer spotted something on the grass and knelt down to pick it up, whereupon Transpique followed suit and went down on one knee, as if he were in a dress rehearsal.

On the day of the visit, everything was in place. Horses were groomed and saddles polished, flowers were arranged and the microphone had been tested and found to work. We were somewhat thrown when we got word that the Princess Royal would be arriving a bit earlier than planned. My nerves had been on edge for weeks and I nearly had a fit because our timings had been worked out to the second. But in fact, it didn't matter at all. Willie Carson pressed ahead and handed out the certificates, talking briefly to each child and praising their achievements. Hilary had explained to them what a brilliantly successful jockey he had been so they were bursting with pride as he shook them by the hand.

After that, everything went to plan. The Princess Royal arrived and toured through the marquee, the classroom and the brand new unsaddling enclosure, asking me a great number of questions about Horse Power and the work we were doing. We returned to the marquee and Michael gave a speech explaining how proud we were of all the children who had completed the programme – three hundred in the last year alone – and recounted his dream of expanding into schools throughout the country.

Richard Erven accompanied the Princess Royal up to the podium, where she unveiled a plaque. Everyone stood as she went back out to her car, and she was obviously delighted when Transpique knelt down before her. He had never been a memorable winner on the racecourse, so it was wonderful that he could have his moment of glory now.

And then it was all over. After all the weeks of careful planning and sleepless nights as I worried about everything that could possibly go wrong, the time just flew past. No horses panicked at the noise and the crowds; no children got upset because they had been kept waiting too long; and the microphone had worked as well. We could relax and open the champagne.

'I knew you were wound up,' Maddy told me, 'because during Michael's speech you kept frowning every time he rustled his papers.'

It's true. I'd been worried that the microphone made the sound of his papers deafening but seemingly no one else had noticed.

There were several old friends there and, as we celebrated, we got to reminiscing about some of the characters who had passed through Greatwood over the years. Back in Devon, there was my lovely Poppy who thought she was a goat and used to get scratches on her nose from picking brambles, following the lead of Angie, the real goat. We laughed about Potentate chasing all the other horses out of the field shelter, something he still does to this day. Michael reminded me of a horse called Devon Dawn, who used to pick up sticks and run round the field with them, for all the world as if he were a dog. There were the old boys such as Sunny and Eddy that had lost their teeth and consequently sprayed everyone in sight with food as they slurped it down, so that their stable ended up looking like a disreputable old folks' home. And, of course, there was that historic moment when Sophie met Darcy Day and sparked the idea that would become the Horse Power programme.

There had been many very difficult moments over the years, as I nursed poorly horses, walking them up and down through the night. And there were all the animals that sadly had to be put down. I've done more than my fair share of holding a horse's head and talking to it gently as a vet administers a lethal injection. Every time, my heart is breaking, but it's all part and parcel of being a responsible carer for animals.

For Michael and me, there have been low points and high points. Money has never stopped being a cause of stress, and during the recession of 2009 our charitable donations dropped off significantly as people tightened their belts. We were back to living on tick and sadly had to let some of the staff go, but we've got our fingers crossed that the economic gloom will lift before too long. The problem is that just when donations drop, the need for our services becomes even greater as people have money worries and can't afford to keep their horses. We can only struggle on and hope we sail out of the doldrums before too long.

The high points have been when we see the changes Greatwood has made to the lives of both the retired race-horses that come to us and the many hundreds of children, from all different backgrounds, and with a wide range of different needs. Horse Power was Michael's idea. He, too, was the one with the vision to approach independent schools with a view to spreading it throughout the country, and I'll never stop admiring his dogged determination to make it all happen.

When you are working hard day in, day out, you don't have time to sit back and reflect on it all, but I know that what we have done here is unique. I'm not aware of any other charity with a programme for racehorses and children with special needs, from which a significant number of the children are able to gain accredited certificates. Often for the first time in their lives, these children find something they enjoy doing, and many of them become so enraptured that they decide they want to go on and work with animals in their careers, or choose to enter the world of racing.

Greatwood seems to engage a part of the brains of children with special needs that no one has reached before. It brings a sparkle, the child is changed, and their parents and schools are delighted.

For the last three years some researchers from Southampton University have been investigating the

'Greatwood effect' to try to pin down how the communication between the animals and the children works. So far all they've shown for sure is that there *is* a reaction and that it makes a difference to the children's lives. But what exactly causes it? We await further results with interest.

In 2008, I was astonished to hear that I'd been nominated for a Betfair Pride of Racing Award, which is given to people who have made a significant contribution to the Racing Industry. Nigel Bunter of Barbury Castle was sponsoring a table at the awards ceremony in London and invited Michael and me to join him, along with some of the charity's trustees. There were a number of awards, for trainers, yard staff and so forth, and I had no expectations of winning anything because it's known to be fiercely competitive, so when my name was called out, I sat with my mouth wide open in shock.

I eventually got my act together and made my way to the front, and I was presented with a bronze statue of a racehorse by the Princess Royal. In one of those awful heart-stopping moments I handed it over to someone else and it dropped to the floor with a heavy thud. An ear was bent, a couple of legs went wonky and it would never be the same again – but I didn't mind. It almost seemed fitting that my damaged award should act as a lasting memory of the type of horses I have helped. We've mended it so it is as good as new and given it pride of place in the cottage.

In fact, I think it's odd to single out individuals for awards. Awards are strange things anyway, with people who do similar jobs set against each other; it's almost like choosing between Brie and Camembert. The kind of work we do is always a team effort. Personally, I couldn't have achieved as much as I have without the amazing team we've built at Greatwood. It's a hard life working with horses, especially in winter, and most yard workers in racing only last a year or two before moving on, but everyone who comes to Greatwood wants to stay, and that makes me very proud.

Our family have all been very supportive of this eccentric life we lead. Michael's son Dan comes to every single event we hold to give us a hand. Clare picked up the love of animals and has now become a vet, although unfortunately she doesn't live close enough to give us free consultations about our animals. Michael's grandchildren, William and Alex, who used to pick the names of our foals, are at university now but they'll come along to the Greatwood Hurdle and our open day every year, even though we occasionally ask them to stand in as car-parking attendants. And each December we have a big family party that everyone attends – but we steer clear of Christmas Day itself since that disastrous Christmas down in Devon when I forgot that children need to be allowed to open their Christmas presents.

I can't believe how fortunate I am with the life we've carved out here. It's challenging, and distressing at times, but I get to live my life surrounded by some extraordinary animals, and that's what makes me tick, as it has done ever since I first learned to ride Tam O'Shanter at the age of four. The fact that we manage to do some good for others along the way is the icing on the cake.

Chapter 24

Amy and Monty

It is fitting that the last chapter in this book should concern one of our biggest success stories, and the one that seems set to open up a new direction for Greatwood in the future. It concerns a girl called Amy, who first came to us three years ago, when she was fourteen years old. I still have a vivid picture of her creeping out of the car, so terrified that she was unable even to say the word 'hello' to Hilary, who had come out to meet her.

Amy had endured a difficult time in her childhood. The trouble started when she had to move primary schools at a young age and was separated from the friends she had made at the last one. She felt shy starting a new school and she was bullied by certain cruel, thoughtless kids, who poked fun at her mother and her and called them names. It also meant that she slipped behind her classmates in the basics, such as learning to read and do sums. The family moved to Wiltshire and at the age of seven Amy was taken into care and separated from her older brothers and sister, after her mother could no longer cope because of domestic violence at home.

Amy was enrolled at a good secondary school and placed with some wonderful foster parents, who soon made her feel part of their large extended family, but all the disruption had taken its toll. She had become a very shy, withdrawn child with a genuine terror of meeting strangers. She would clam up completely in front of anyone she didn't know, and was particularly scared of men, because of the history of violence in her family. Her fear was so great that even when she really wanted to buy something in a shop she was unable to summon the courage to go up to the counter to pay for it. If she had to take a bus, she would be in tears when she had to open her mouth to ask for a ticket. Unsurprisingly, she lacked any concentration when it came to schoolwork and she was so far behind her classmates that she couldn't see the point in trying.

Amy's only passion in life was horses. A stepfather had told her all about them, and she'd caught the bug. She tried riding at local stables a couple of times but couldn't handle it because of all the strangers there. People she didn't know scared her more than the horses enchanted her, and she couldn't force herself to do it. Instead she hung some horse posters in her bedroom and resorted to daydreams of a world in which she would one day work solely with horses and wouldn't need to have anything to do with human beings at all.

A teacher at Amy's school suggested that she should come to Greatwood to do our Horse Power course, because she thought it might help her to open up and make it easier for her to handle new experiences. Amy was terrified because she realised it would involve meeting strangers, but at the same time was curious to meet our Thoroughbreds and was interested in the rescue work we did. Her foster mother, Debbie, drove her over for her first visit, and Amy's legs were shaking as she got out of the car, but once they reached the classroom, Hilary's quiet manner soon put her at ease.

Amy watched a PowerPoint presentation about Greatwood, and then they went for a walk round the farm where she met some of the best-known characters amongst our horses – Potentate and Deano's Beano, Steady Eddy and Monty. As she stroked them, Hilary noticed that her nails were bitten painfully down to the quicks. If any other members of staff seemed as if they were going to come her way, she would bite her lip so hard it looked as though she would draw blood, but she didn't show the slightest sign of nerves around the towering horses. She was quite happy to get up close, pet them and whisper to them. They took to her as well, and there seemed to be a particular spark between her and Monty.

Monty was the old-timer from Devon who had taken care of Sunny and Eddy when they returned to us, becoming part of an eccentric threesome. Sad times came when Sunny's health deteriorated to the point where we had no choice but to put him to sleep. We were all devastated. I think everyone working in the yard was in tears and I let the staff go home early that day. Steady Eddy took it hardest, though. He called out for Sunny for hours on end and was palpably distressed at losing his friend of the last fifteen years. Monty paced around pulling anxious faces and grieving in his own way.

I had an idea though. Just a short time before this, a new horse called Chief Runner had been brought to us. He was twenty-six years old, with bad cataracts, and was obviously vulnerable. He had one particular idiosyncrasy, which was deafening us with his shrill cries for food at mealtimes. He found the other horses in the yard intimidating but a few days after Sunny died, we put him in the stable with Eddy and Monty, and they appeared to strike up an immediate friendship.

Still, we were worried about putting Runner out into a field with a large herd when the summer months came, but we needn't have been concerned, because it was Monty to the rescue! Just as he had done when Sunny and Eddy arrived, Monty positioned himself protectively between Runner and the rest of the herd. If any other horse came near, he circled and kicked out in a threatening manner, letting them know that Runner was his friend, and we never had a moment's trouble with them. A new threesome was formed, of Monty, Eddy and Runner, and they became as inseparable as the previous threesome with Sunny.

Amy was touched by the story of Monty protecting other vulnerable horses. She met him again during her second visit when she was mucking out the goats and he popped his head over the partition to see what was going on. She gave him a cuddle and their friendship was sealed. Hilary taught her how to groom him and she found out that he liked music, so she would turn on a radio and sing to him as she brushed his coat. He frequently fell asleep in her arms, which is the biggest sign of trust a horse can offer.

From that point on, Amy blossomed. Gradually she overcame her fear and was able to talk to the rest of the staff – Sue, Robbie, Maddy, Edward and me – without biting her lip or trying to hide behind Hilary. She was a caring girl, who got upset about the condition of rescue horses and was very loving towards the animals.

She and Hilary became very close, and Amy confided in her about the difficulties she faced at home and at school. 'I can't believe I used to be scared of you when I first came!' she exclaimed. 'You're not at all scary. I feel silly for worrying now.'

As week followed week we saw that little girl come out of her shell and we found out that she had a cheeky, fun-loving side.

'That's why you get on with Monty,' Robbie exclaimed. 'It's because you're both cheeky.'

'Who, me?' she grinned. 'Can't think what you mean!'

Amy threw herself into the ten-week course, helping with the chickens, geese, sheep and goats, as well as the horses, and she was one of the children who were given their certificate by Willie Carson and were there to see the Princess Royal unveiling the plaque in the unsaddling enclosure. She went back to school afterwards, knowing there was something in the world she was good at and that she'd made new friends. Her teacher rang to say she couldn't believe the difference. Amy was answering questions in class, taking part in group activities, and seemed happier chatting to her friends at break times as well. She was like a new person.

The following year, when she was fifteen, Amy came back to Greatwood to do a two-week work-experience placement on the farm, and everyone was very impressed with her efforts.

'It's good having someone you can trust to get the job done,' Robbie said, 'especially when we're at our busiest.'

'You only need to tell her something once,' Sue commented. 'She never forgets an instruction.'

Amy was working out in the yard now rather than in the classroom and Sue took her under her wing. It transpired that they had very similar backgrounds and had confronted many of the same difficulties when they were younger. Sue was a great role model in that respect because she had overcome all her earlier problems to build a successful career in racehorse welfare, and is now married with a baby on the way. She is living proof that life can change for the better. I think working together helped both Amy and Sue because it made them realise that they are not alone, and they have become very close.

When Amy turned sixteen, she was quite clear about what she wanted to do on leaving school.

'I want to work with horses,' she said. 'In a place just like Greatwood, where they help to rescue animals.'

Debbie, her foster mum, got in touch with Haddon Training, a well-known organisation for training people to work with horses, which can offer NVQ (National Vocational Qualification) training and apprenticeship programmes. These are hands-on, practical qualifications. You don't need to write scores of essays and pass written exams, but you do need to know about every single aspect of horse care.

The staff at Haddon Training were happy to help Amy but they needed to find a location where she could be employed for a year so she could learn on the job.

'Erm, there's this place I know called Greatwood ...' Amy suggested.

Phone calls were made, and straight away we said we'd love to have her. We all liked Amy and wanted her to do well, and if we could help further her chosen career choice, we would, despite the fact that she would probably need a lot of guidance. She'd made such a good impression during her work experience that we knew she would be an asset – and that's the way it has proved. She works tirelessly, dealing with every aspect of the horses' daily care, from feeding to grooming to leading them around from stable to field and holding them so that visiting children with special needs can groom and stroke them. You can tell she's enjoying herself. If you walk past the stable, you can often hear her singing while she works.

She's doing all kinds of things she would never have been able to do three years ago. Every morning she gets herself up at 6am and shares a car to work with Sue and Paul, another staff member, whereas she would never have been able to get into a car with a man before. In the summer she went camping with her foster mum's brother Sam and helped to look after his children. And she has even volunteered to hand out leaflets about Greatwood at the next Cheltenham Open, which will require a confidence no one who knew her three years ago would ever have imagined she possessed.

Michael and I are delighted with the way it's all worked out. To train young people and help them earn qualifications that will enable them to join the workforce seems like the logical way forward for us. We hadn't explored it specifically before, so we're grateful to Amy for suggesting it and being such a model first placement.

We have plans to spread Greatwood Horse Power throughout the country and possibly overseas as well.

Over the coming years, we'd like to see hundreds more racehorses coming to Greatwood, either to retrain for a second career or to enjoy a comfortable retirement in our fields, where they can interact with hundreds of youngsters wearing purple Greatwood sweatshirts, with muck on their wellies and straw in their hair, smelling of horses and goats, and having experiences that could well change the course of their young lives.

Find out more
about Greatwood

There's information about our work and photographs of some of the horses at our website:

www.greatwoodcharity.org

If you would like to make a donation to help us with the work we are doing, you can do so through the website.

If you cannot make a donation online, then please download our Donation & Gift Aid form and post it to us at:

Greatwood
Rainscombe Hill Farm
Clench Common
Marlborough
Wiltshire SN8 4DT

Alternatively, call us on 01672 514535 (Monday to Friday, 8:30am to 4:30pm) to process your donation. We accept all major debit/credit cards.

Your donations will be even more valuable to us (at no extra cost to you) if you complete a gift aid declaration form. Providing you pay tax of an equivalent amount or more, you can reclaim 28p for every £1 you donate. It's a big help, so thank you. If you pay higher rate tax, you can reclaim the difference through your tax return.

You could also donate shares or land to Greatwood. Perhaps just a small holding of shares that are not worth selling because it would cost more than they are worth, or a larger share holding or piece of land. It's another tax-efficient way of helping us.

Or why not become a Friend of Greatwood? You'll receive:

- a newsletter with updates on the progress of all the horses, the ones recently rescued and the ones successfully rehomed
- free entry to the Greatwood Open Day
- special offers for race meetings

Most importantly, a Friend of Greatwood knows they are making a genuine difference to the horses we help and the children that attend our programmes throughout the year.

THANK YOU!

Acknowledgements

The success of Greatwood is dependent upon all those who have so generously supported us, and my special thanks must go to our Trustees, Jeremy Hummerstone, Alison Cocks and Richard Powell, who have stuck with us through thick and thin, and also to Elizabeth Frearson, David Hillyard, Martin Featherston Godley and Stephen Williams, who have so generously and unstintingly given their time and expertise in guiding us to where we stand today. We have been lucky that our Patrons have lent their name to us, and are grateful to Kim Bailey, Nigel Bunter, Nicky Henderson, the Hon. Harry Herbert, John Jarvis CVO CBE, Jodie Kidd, Rachel King, John and Jenny McCririck, Brian Stewart-Brown, Peter Walwyn and Lady Whent. Lady Whent has supported us as both Trustee and Patron and has been such a help to me in guiding me through difficult horse welfare issues.

Huge thanks must go to all those within the Racing Industry, and I would like to thank all at Retraining of Racehorses who have supported us since its inception in 2000. It is largely due to them that Greatwood has been able to continue with its work with ex-racehorses. The original Chairman, Brigadier Andrew Parker Bowles OBE, helped us right from the very beginning, ably assisted by Di Arbuthnot. Their work in spreading the word about the versatility of the racehorse has meant that now hundreds of racehorses are retrained for rewarding careers after their racing days are over.

I acknowledge with gratitude all the hundreds of carers who have so generously taken on our horses and the thousands of supporters and friends who have helped us over the years, and of course all our volunteers. In particular our thanks go to Stan Criticos, Nigel and Penny Bunter for sponsoring The Greatwood Hurdle, Jeff Herrington WHW, Peter and Greta Craker and the late Jim Weeden.

There are many sections within racing that have stepped in to support us: the trainers who have given us their time and kindly offered mornings on the gallops as auction lots; all those who have donated wonderful prizes for our big fundraising events, and the Funding Trusts that have generously donated to our cause. We would also like to thank Ladbrokes, Bet365, Blue Square, William

Hill, Stan James, WBX, Northern Racing plc, Matt Doyle at Sky Bet, Paddy Power and OLBG, all at the racecourses, especially Edward Gillespie, Peter McNeile and Simon Claisse at Cheltenham, Caroline Fleming, Lisa Ward, Maddy White and Stephen Higgins at Newbury, Jenny Cheshire at Worcester, Wincanton, Ascot and Nicky Sneddon at Sandown, and Sarah Oliver at the Amateur Jockeys Association.

Thank you to Peter Clarke who has kindly sponsored a race in our name every year at Newbury, Weatherbys, Nick Cheyne, Theresa Meredith, Di Harvey, who helps us with passports, Holly Hawker and Kim Langeslag, and to our supporters in the media: Andrew Franklin at Channel4 Racing, Tanya Stevenson, Al Plunkett, John and Jenny McCririck, Luke Harvey, Nick Luck, Rishi Persad, Dr Willie Carson OBE, the *Racing Post*, Mick and Chloe Fitzgerald, Chanelle McCoy, Richard Erven and Wooden Spoon, Mike Cattermole, Matt Chapman, John Francome, Richard Phillips, Jacko Fanshaw, Lynda Ramsden, Clare Balding, Attheraces and RUK. Our thanks also go to Jilly Cooper, Jodie Kidd, Keeneland, Kim Bailey, Henry Hannon, Alan and Rachel King, Chris Vine, Fiona Crick, Annabel and Howard Spooner, Guy and Fi Sangster, Dr Ian and Hilary Abrahams, Jeremy Sumbler of Covered Occasions, Dermot de Courcy Robinson, Julia Langton, Gillian Flanagan, Sandy Briddon, Johnny Ferrand, Spike and Marion Clarke, Elite Racing Club, Tony Hill and Jane Lock.

We are so grateful to Marlborough Horse Transport (Nicky and Dean, who practically drop everything to pick up horses for us in an emergency), Ben Clarke, Edward Maurice, the Vigar Smiths, James, who has expertly made our haylage and hay each year and has helped us in many emergencies, Lorraine Perry, Bill and Jennie Simpson, Lesley and Russell Field, Charlton Baker, Philip Evans, Scott Sartin, Richard and Anne Lavelle, Tara Economakis, Reg and Linkie Whitehead, Andi Cunningham, Lisa Lavia, Kate Williams, Vicky Smart, Yvonne Jacques, Beryl Jones, Lionel Mill, Gavin James, Miss Brokenbrow, Stephen and Pepita Hurd, Tessa Woodhouse, Carrie Humble, our vets Richard Gillatt and Andrew McGonnell, Rob, Dick and Marilyn Evans, our farriers Nick Rule and Consultant Andrew Poynton.

I would like to thank my mother for making acres of purple cloths and providing flowers and food for events, Freddie Day-Robinson who drove to Greatwood from Sussex three times a week for years to work in the office, Matt Day-Robinson, Kate, Paul, William and Alex Green, Tod and Dan Yeadon for attending and supporting us at practically every event, Sally Yeadon, Clare Yeadon who ran our Open Days, and all the dedicated people who work with us and have worked for us in the past.

Our equine team is extraordinary; their level of expertise in looking after the horses is second to none and together we have been through many happy and sad times. Part of animal welfare involves making difficult decisions and our staff have always been incredibly supportive during difficult times. All our staff past and present have made a huge contribution to the success of Greatwood: Susie Dennis, Sam Ricks, Gary Evans, Sue Danaher, our gifted Equine Welfare Manager, Robbie Neville, Becky Lyons, Paul Alder, Lucie and Coudy Cecil, Dan Malek, Amy Howell, Jon Baron, Karen Hall, Hettie Thomas, Mikey Saunders, Melanie Gee and all the teaching staff who have helped hundreds of children over the years.

And finally, massive thanks to Maddy Peake, who has been with us for five years and has guided the charity in every circumstance and adversity.